THE A-Z OF CURIOUS
LONDON

THE A-Z OF CURIOUS

LONDON

GILLY PICKUP

The
History
Press

This book is dedicated to my beloved mother, Janet Reekie, who passed away while I was writing it. She would have been proud and, like me, she loved London too.

First published 2013

The History Press
The Mill, Brimscombe Port
Stroud, Gloucestershire, GL5 2QG
www.thehistorypress.co.uk

British Library Cataloguing in Publication Data.
A catalogue record for this book is available from the British Library.

ISBN 978 0 7524 8968 1

Typesetting and origination by The History Press
Printed and bound in Great Britain by
Marston Book Services Limited, Oxfordshire

Contents

Acknowledgements

THANK YOU to London, the greatest city in the world, because, without her bottomless wealth of stories, history and characters, this book would not exist.

Thank you to Matilda, my commissioning editor, for putting enough trust in me to write *The A-Z of Curious London*, and everyone whose enthusiasm and encouragement helped to keep the pages flowing. My appreciation also goes to all those who, when they found out I was writing this book said, 'Oh, how exciting! Let me know when it's finished and I'll go and buy a copy'. Now's your chance!

I am grateful for the images received from various sources – credits are given with each individual image used – and I would also like to thank the photographers whose work is made available through Wikimedia Commons, again I have listed details with each image.

Grateful thanks to Sydney, Lester and most of all, my husband Mike, for help, advice, ideas, and endless cups of invigorating coffee. Mike's suggestions and support have been invaluable.

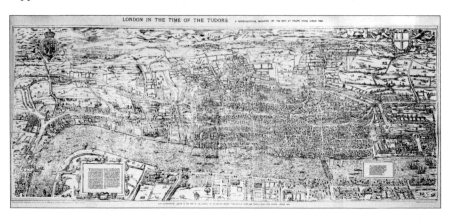

London, *c.* 1590. (Maps of old London ed. G.E. Milton. (1908 author Ralph Agas from Wikimedia Commons)

Introduction

THIS BOOK is full of spooky, gruesome, weird but true things about one of the world's greatest cities. I have tried to bring the past to life and keep the present interesting in this compendium, a book to dip into when the mood takes you, or read from A to Z if you prefer. Although it includes a lot of history, it does not dwell on the boring bits. So, if you want to trawl through pages and pages of serious history, this is not the book for you. My advice is to treat it as a fun companion. Brimming full of stories to astonish, amuse and inform – some of London's best-kept secrets are unravelled in these pages.

London is a particularly rich source of strange tales: from the gruesome (why did a dentist keep his dead wife on view in a shop window?); the bizarre

View over London. (© VisitBritain / James McCormick)

Piccadilly Circus around 1890–1900. (Library of Congress, LC-DIG-ppmsca-08577)

(a doctor who treated epilepsy by firing a gun near to his patients to frighten the illness away); the quirky (a 4,000-year-old mouse made from Nile clay); the seriously grisly (the murderer who drank his victims' blood before dissolving them in acid); the naughty (the Queen who showed an ambassador her bare bosom); the scary (the tube station where the blood-curdling screams of an eighteenth-century murder victim have been heard); and the simply peculiar (the dance you would definitely never, ever, ever want to do).

To sum up, you will read of eccentrics, legends, murders, scandals, ghosts, incredible characters, weird historical facts and yarns galore. I was sorry when I reached my allotted word count, because there are so many more tales to tell about this extraordinary city. Those included only just scratch the surface. I hope you enjoy reading *The A–Z of Curious London* as much as I have enjoyed writing it.

Gilly Pickup, 2013

The A-Z of Curious London

❧ ARRESTED FOR WEARING A TOP HAT ❧

London haberdasher James Hetherington was arrested on the Strand in 1797 for wearing a top hat. In fact, he caused a terrible commotion as no one had ever seen a hat like it before, and according to a newspaper of the day, '… passers-by panicked, women fainted and children screamed'. It is even said that a boy suffered a broken arm when he was knocked down in the hullabaloo. Hetherington was charged with causing a breach of the peace by 'appearing on the public highway wearing a tall structure of shining lustre … calculated to disturb timid people'. You could say that was the beginning of something big as far as headgear went and, after the tumult subsided, people started to place orders for top hats. It reached its heyday in the nineteenth century, when it was said that an assembled gathering of gentlemen looked like the chimneys of the Industrial Revolution!

Whilst on the subject of hats, the world's oldest family-run hat shop was founded in London in 1676. Around this time, after the Great Plague and Fire of London caused havoc in the City, well-to-do families and tradesmen started to move westwards. In medieval times, the City constituted most of London, but over the years the conurbation grew far beyond it. As the City's boundaries have remained almost unchanged since the Middle Ages, it is now only a tiny part of the metropolis, although it holds city status in its own right.

Soon the development of the West End had begun, encouraged by landowners who had lost heavily during the English Civil War and needed to raise money from their estates. George James Lock was one of these tradesmen. The patriarchal head of the Lock family was Sir John Lock and they

The Strand, *c.* 1901. (Library of Congress, LC-USZ62-68658)

had interests in coffee, chocolate and tobacco imported from Turkey. When the Great Fire of 1666 disrupted the business, the family moved to the West End. In 1686, funded by his successful trading concerns, George James Lock became the leaseholder of seven houses in St James's Street. On the site there had once stood a real tennis court built in 1617 for the then Prince of Wales, who became Charles I. George lived in one of the houses, and rented the other houses out to merchants and private individuals.

The bowler hat was created at James Lock's business in 1850, for a progressive farmer from Norfolk called William Coke. It was a domed hat, hardened by the application of shellac, designed to protect the heads of gamekeepers from overhanging branches. The hat was a snug fit to ensure that it would not easily blow or fall off. The prototype was made by Southwark hat makers, Thomas and

William Bowler, and was brought to St James's Street to be tested by William Coke himself. He did this by jumping on the hat and, satisfied that it withstood his weight, he purchased it.

The Lock & Co. shop has supplied headgear to the great and the good including Oscar Wilde, Napoleon, Winston Churchill, Frank Sinatra and Johnny Depp. The shop has been at 6 St James's Street (SW1) since the mid-1700s and was even patronised by Admiral Lord Nelson, who bought his first hat from Lock's in 1800. It was made of beaver fur with a black silk cockade and cost £1 11s 6d. He became a frequent customer and later purchased a black silk hat for an unnamed lady, almost certainly his mistress, Emma Hamilton.

In 1803, he returned to the shop. The glare of reflected light from the sea and the battle hazards of smoke and grit were affecting his good eye, and he was worried that he would lose the sight in that one too. He asked if the shop could make him a hat with a built-in shade, protecting both eyes. Lock & Co. made him two hats to this specification and the drawings survive today in the shop's archives.

The phrase 'mad as a hatter' was not just a fictional invention of Lewis Carroll's *Alice in Wonderland*. Mad hatter disease, caused by inhaling toxic fumes from mercury nitrate, a chemical used in the felting process, affected the nervous system. Besides the damage it caused to the lungs, the fumes also affected the brain, leading to paralysis, loss of memory, mental health problems and eventual death. Unfortunately, hat workers did not get much sympathy in the nineteenth century as victims tended to be mocked and regarded as drunkards; they had a reputation for liking a drink to quench the thirst caused by the dust and fumes of their occupation.

⚜ BEER, BEER, GLORIOUS BEER ⚜

The London Beer Flood took place at Meux's Brewery on the junction of Tottenham Court Road and Oxford Street, on 17 October 1814. A 22-foot high porter vat of around 512,000 litres of beer ruptured, causing a chain reaction with surrounding vats. The beer tsunami destroyed two houses and knocked down the wall of the Tavistock Arms pub in Great Russell Street, trapping fourteen-year-old employee, Eleanor Cooper, under the rubble.

The Times of 19 October reported:

> The neighbourhood of St Giles was thrown into the utmost consternation on Monday night, by one of the most melancholy accidents we ever remember. About six o'clock, one of the vats in the extensive premises of Messrs Henry Meux and Co., in Banbury-street, St Giles burst, and in a moment New-street, George-street and several others in the vicinity were deluged with the contents, amounting to 3,500 barrels of strong beer. The fluid, in its course, swept everything before it. Two houses in New-street, adjoining the brewhouse, were totally demolished. The inhabitants, who were of the poorer class, were all at home.

The paper went on to describe the accident:

> The bursting of the brew-house walls, and the fall of heavy timber, materially contributed to aggravate the mischief, by forcing the roofs and walls of the adjoining houses. Many of the cellars on the south side of Russell street are completely inundated with beer; and in some houses the inhabitants had to save themselves from drowning by mounting their highest pieces of furniture.

It was a terrible tragedy, but some impoverished locals saw it as a bit of good fortune and in an effort to obtain some free beer they ran to the scene carrying pots, pans, kettles and anything else they could use to scoop it up. Some of the more desperate locals simply threw themselves on the ground to lap it up.

As the tide receded, the true damage became known. Nine people were dead; some were drowned while others had been swept away in the flood and died of injuries they sustained. One man died days later from alcohol poisoning – such was his heroic attempt to stem the tide by drinking as much beer as he could.

In a bid to make some money from the terrible event, relatives of the deceased decided to exhibit their families' corpses in their homes and charge a viewing fee. This led to yet more disaster when too many people crowded in to one house, causing the floor to collapse and plunging all of the visitors into a cellar half full of beer.

The brewery was eventually taken to court over the accident, but the disaster was ruled as an 'act of god', leaving no one responsible. However, the company found it difficult to cope with the financial aftermath of the disaster, with a significant loss of sales made worse because they had already paid duty on the beer. Fortunately,

Beer poster. (© VisitLondon images/ britainonview / Ingrid Rasmussen)

the brewery was able to continue trading after a successful application to Parliament allowed them to reclaim the duty.

❧ BLOW-BLADDER STREET TO FRYING PAN ALLEY ❧

Well, after all, what's in a name? Plenty it seems. After the Norman invasion of 1066, most of London's business was conducted in what is now the City of London, otherwise known as the Square Mile, so-called because it was just over one square mile in area. The City is the world's leading financial and business centre, and has the unusual ratio of forty times more workers than it has residents. None of the Square Mile's thoroughfares were called 'road' until comparatively recent boundary changes – even City Road can be said to lead to the city, rather than entering it!

Many medieval street names tended to reflect the function or economic activity that took place there; 'Cornhill' was where the corn market was located. 'Cheapside' was the main street and site of one of the principal produce markets in London, 'cheap' roughly translated as 'market' in medieval English. In those days, the royal processional route from the Tower of London to the Palace of Westminster went through Cheapside, and during State occasions, the conduits here flowed with wine. Unsurprisingly, the masses flocked here to linger and enjoy boozy revelries.

During Edward III's reign in the fourteenth century, tournaments took place in adjacent fields and the dangers were not limited to the participants. In 1330, a wooden stand built to accommodate Queen Philippa and her companions collapsed during a tournament to celebrate the birth of the Black Prince. There were no casualties, but the King was furious and if the Queen had not intervened, the stand's builders would have been 'put to death'.

Seventeenth-century poet and author of *Paradise Lost*, John Milton, was born in Bread Street, named such because of the produce sold there. Similarly, there is a Milk Street and Poultry Street. Frying Pan Alley was part of a notorious East End slum district in the nineteenth century, home to braziers and ironmongers who hung frying pans outside their premises as a way of advertising their

Knight on a horse. (© L Moyse)

businesses. Honey Lane was full of beekeepers selling their wares, until it was destroyed in the Great Fire of 1666. The site later became home to Honey Lane Market and was home to over a hundred butchers' stalls. In 1782, C.P. Moritz wrote, 'Nothing in London makes a more detestable sight than the butchers' stalls. The guts and other refuse are all thrown on the street and set up an unbearable stink.' A worse sight would have greeted him in 1517, when butcher John Pynkard was paraded around London wearing four sides of rotten meat and a sign reading 'For putting to sale stynkyng bacon'.

Then there was Stew Lane, where you might expect to find a tasty casserole to tuck into, but this street was simply packed to the gunnels with brutal and bawdy brothels, which were called 'stews' because of their origins as houses with heated rooms used for hot air or vapour baths.

Centuries passed and the west of the City started to see more development. After his Restoration in 1660, Charles II gave away swathes of land in Mayfair to those who had supported him. Albemarle Street, Jermyn Street and Berkeley Square commemorate Restoration courtiers, while Arlington Street was named after the Earl of Arlington, Sir Henry Bennet, whose job was to acquire and manage the royal mistresses. This was no easy task when serving Charles II, who was known to have more than one mistress at a time and did not keep his fourteen illegitimate children a secret.

Blow-Bladder Street was called such because it was where vendors would hang inflated bladders on poles for sale. Thankfully, bladder sellers left in 1720, and the more genteel seamstresses and milliners moved in. It is now called King Edward Street.

In 1738, a highwayman, who had carried out robberies on Finchley Common, was chased to London. When he thought he had lost his pursuers, he stopped at a public house in Burlington Gardens near Piccadilly, but it was not long before he realised he was still being followed. He galloped through Hyde Park and was followed to Fulham Fields, where he realised he had no way of escaping. The highwayman threw his ill-gotten gains to peasants at work in the fields, telling them 'they would soon witness the end of an unfortunate man'. He then pulled out his pistol and shot himself. He was buried at the crossroads and the area became 'Purser's Cross'.

Spitalfields originated when Walter Brune founded a large hospital for poor brethren of the order of St Austin in the fields east of Bishopsgate in 1197. The surrounding pastures were called Hospital-fields, but cockney slang dropped the first two letters to form the name 'Spitalfields'.

Crummier areas included Addle Street – the word 'addle' meant 'urine' or 'liquid filth' – still survives today, as does Fetter Lane. The latter was derived from 'Fewterer' meaning 'idle, disorderly person'. Other street names have been renamed in deference to present-day attitudes. Take Sherborne Lane, which was known as Shitteborwelane then later Shite-burn lane in the 1200s, possibly due to nearby cess pits. Pissing Alley, one of several identically named streets whose names survived the Great Fire of London was renamed the more polite Little Friday Street in 1848, before being absorbed into Cannon Street in 1853–54. Petticoat Lane, the meaning of which is sometimes misinterpreted as being related to prostitution – it was actually named after the Huguenot lacemakers – was renamed Middlesex Street in 1830.

⚜ BOILED ALIVE FOR POISONING THE SOUP ⚜

In 1531, the Bishop of Rochester's cook, Richard Roose, was boiled to death at Smithfield. He had confessed to poisoning soup served to Bishop John Fisher and his guests. The Bishop survived, but some of his guests, presumably those who had more than one helping, died.

The 1531 'Acte for Poysoning' says,

On the Eighteenth day of February, 1531, one Richard Roose, of Rochester, Cook, also called Richard Cooke, did cast poison into a vessel of yeast to baum, standing in the kitchen of the Bishop of Rochester's Palace, at Lambeth March, by means of which two persons who happened to eat of the pottage made with such yeast died.

Some believed that Anne Boleyn was responsible, saying that she and her family had bribed Roose to poison the soup to get rid of Fisher, but Henry VIII did not believe this to be the case. It is definitely a possibility, because the Bishop was in opposition to Henry's Church reforms and his plan to divorce Catherine of Aragon in order to marry Anne.

Following Roose's arrest, an Act was passed specifically to deal with his case. From then on, poisoning would be deemed an act of high treason and anyone found guilty would be boiled to death. Roose was executed in this manner and the unfortunate cook took several hours to die.

The Chronicle of the Grey Friars of London (1531) announced:

This yere was a coke boylyd in a cauderne in Smythfeld for he wolde a powsyned the bishop of Rochester Fycher with dyvers of hys servanttes, and he was lockyd in a chayne and pullyd up and downe with a gybbyt at dyvers tymes tyll he was dede.

The gruesome Act was repealed under Henry VIII's son, Edward VI.

BUCKINGHAM HOUSE:
❧ SCENE OF SUFFRAGETTES ❧
AND GANDHI'S LOIN-CLOTH

After the Norman Conquest, the site of Buckingham House was passed to Geoffrey de Mandeville, who donated it to the monks of Westminster Abbey. It is thought that the first house to be erected on the site belonged to Sir William Blake. Previously known as Goring House and Arlington House, it was named Buckingham House after the eighteenth-century Tory politician, John Sheffield (3rd Earl of Mulgrave and Marquess of Normanby) who was given the title of Duke of Buckingham in 1703. He built Buckingham House for himself as a grand London home.

A little further down the line, George III purchased the house in 1762 for his wife Queen Charlotte to use as a family home close to St James's Palace, where the many court functions were held. Buckingham House was known as the Queen's House and fourteen of George III's fifteen children were born there. In 1826, the unpopular George IV decided to transform the house into a palace, although it seems he never moved in. Even though the Duke of Wellington

Buckingham Palace. (© britainonview)

described George and his brothers as 'the damnedest millstones about the neck of any government that may be imagined', he generously offered the palace as a new home for Parliament when the Palace of Westminster was destroyed by fire in 1834. However, his offer was declined.

Queen Victoria, whose first name was actually Alexandrina, was the first monarch to take up residence in July 1837 and, in June 1838, she was the first British sovereign to leave from Buckingham Palace for a coronation. Her marriage to Prince Albert in 1840 highlighted the palace's shortcomings, including the lack of nurseries for the newly married couple – although obviously George III had not found this to be a problem – and too few guest rooms. The only solution was to move the Marble Arch, which now stands at the north-east corner of Hyde Park, and build a fourth wing, creating a quadrangle. That is the kind of thing you can do if you are a monarch.

The palace certainly has no shortage of rooms these days; there are 775 in total, including nineteen state rooms, fifty-two royal and guest bedrooms, 188 staff bedrooms, ninety-two offices and seventy-eight bathrooms. It also has its own post office, swimming pool, staff cafeteria, doctor's surgery and cinema. Over 800 members of staff are based at the palace, with jobs ranging from housekeeping to horticulture and catering to correspondence. Some of the more unusual jobs include fendersmith, clockmaker and flagman and, because there are more than 350 clocks and watches in the palace, two full-time horological conservators that wind them up every week and keep them in good order.

A cradle belonging to a wealthy family, 1861. (© Victoria & Albert Museum)

The garden includes a helicopter landing area, a lake and a tennis court. Thirty different species of bird live in the garden and more than 350 different varieties of wild flowers flourish in the peaceful setting, of which some are extremely rare. As well as being the venue for summer garden parties, it was the setting for a charity tennis competition in 2000, pop and classical music concerts in 2002, and a children's party featuring a host of characters from popular children's books in 2006.

Edward VII is the only monarch to have been born and to have died at Buckingham Palace. One of his dogs, a terrier named Caesar, outlived the King and walked behind his coffin in the funeral procession. Both Prince Charles and Prince Andrew were born at Buckingham Palace, and notices of Royal births and deaths are still attached to the railings for the public to read, although now they are also announced on the Royal website.

Through the years, many distinguished figures have visited Buckingham Palace since it became the official London residence of the monarchy. Among these were a seven-year-old Wolfgang Amadeus Mozart (when it was still Buckingham House), Felix Mendelssohn, Johann Strauss Junior, Charles Dickens, Alfred Lord Tennyson, Thomas Woodrow Wilson, John F. Kennedy, Mahatma

Gandhi (who is reported to have worn a loin-cloth and sandals to tea with King George V), Neil Armstrong, Laurence Olivier and Nelson Mandela.

Like many historic buildings, Buckingham Palace is reported to have odd phantom or two, one of which is thought to be the ghost of a monk who died in the monastery's punishment cell. He is said to wear heavy chains and to be dressed in brown, but for some reason he only appears on Christmas Day on the terrace over the gardens to the rear of the building. Another ghost reputed to haunt the palace is that of Major John Gwynne, a private secretary to King Edward VII. Fearing disgrace in an upcoming divorce case, he shot himself in his office on the first floor, and members of staff have apparently seen and heard him on various occasions.

Being an iconic building has naturally led to Buckingham Palace being part of many historical moments, giving it an interesting and varied past. In 1914, suffragettes took their cause to Buckingham Palace, and two campaigners chained themselves to the railings in protest, as it was thought that the Royal Family were against women having the right to vote.

Some years later, Buckingham Palace was in the news again, this time when it suffered nine direct bomb hits during the Second World War. There was only one casualty. Police officer Steve Robertson was killed by flying debris whilst on duty at the palace, when the north side was wrecked in March 1941. A plaque in the garden commemorates him.

Secret tunnels under the streets of London connect Buckingham Palace to the Palace of Westminster, which the Queen Mother is reported to have once investigated with King George VI. During their exploration, they discovered a man unknown to them, who claimed to be a friend of a friend who worked in the palace. The Queen Mother is recorded as saying he was 'a Geordie' and 'most courteous'.

In 1608, King James I had a Mulberry Garden planted to the north of the present palace in an attempt to foster the cultivation of silkworms. His idea was to make money by producing silk in England. However, the idea was a non-starter and the Mulberry Garden was turned into a public recreation ground.

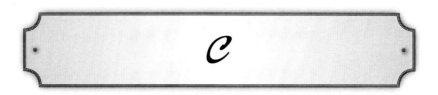

CHURCHILL'S TEETH,
❧ THE GIANT'S SKELETON, ❧
AND AN ENORMOUS TUMOUR

Do you fancy having a gander at Churchill's false teeth? Then visit the Hunterian Museum, housed in the Royal College of Surgeons in Lincoln's Inn Field. As well as holding Churchill's gnashers, it holds a fascinating historical collection amassed by anatomist and surgeon John Hunter (1728–1793). The collection of around 3,500 specimens includes many of Hunter's most famous and fascinating pieces, with an interesting mix of comparative anatomy and pathology specimens. There are full skeletons, skulls, teeth, dried preparations, wax teaching models, historical surgical and dental instruments, paintings, drawings and sculptures.

John Hunter was responsible for moving the medical profession away from barber surgeons and into the world of modern medicine that we know today. He spent time as a doctor in the army and is reported to have developed new methods of treating gunshot wounds. Hunter's professional interests also included studies into the transplantation of teeth. In 1776, he became surgeon to King George III. Many specimens he collected are displayed in glass cabinets. Some of the more horrific include a 10lb tumour, which was removed from the face of a John Burley in 1785, and as if that was not bad enough, it was done so without anaesthetic.

Exhibits include the skeleton of the 7ft 7in-tall 'Irish giant' Charles Byrne, a collection of (pretty gruesome) surgical instruments dating from the seventeenth century; the tooth of a megatherium (an extinct giant sloth) donated by Charles Darwin; and preserved crocodiles and insects. There are carbolic sprays used by Joseph Lister, the pioneer of antiseptic surgery. Before Lister began his work, surgeons did not sterilise their surgical tools, and so it is not surprising that many patients died after being operated on. Mathematician Charles Babbage's brain is also on display, together with teeth retrieved from soldiers on the battlefield of Waterloo and a necklace of human teeth brought from the Congo by explorer Henry Morton Stanley.

Now, getting back to Churchill's dentures, these are housed in a glass case surrounded by many others that once belonged to royalty. Churchill had several sets, which were made by a dental technician called Derek Cudlipp. Cudlipp would recall how, when the Prime Minister was angry, he would remove his dentures and

Hunterian Museum exhibits. (© Hunterian Museum)

throw them across the room. During the Second World War, the severity of the news from the front line was judged by how far the dentures flew.

The collection includes amputation knives and almost every part of the human body that you could wish (or not wish) to see, including the rectum of the Bishop of Durham, Thomas Thurlow, which is in a glass jar. The Bishop died in 1791 and the museum calls the exhibit by its formal name: Object RCSHC/P 192.

CLEOPATRA'S NEEDLE, HAIR PINS, ❖ A BABY'S BOTTLE AND A RAZOR ❖

This ancient Egyptian obelisk is on the Embankment and has absolutely nothing to do with Cleopatra. The Egyptian ruler, Muhammad Ali, donated Cleopatra's Needle to London in 1819 to commemorate the victory of Lord Horatio Nelson at the Battle of the Nile in 1801 and the victory of Sir Ralph Abercromby the same year at the Battle of Alexandria. Both victories were part of the French Revolutionary Wars.

The enormous cost of transporting Cleopatra's Needle to London could not initially be justified by the British Government and so the great obelisk did not arrive in Britain until 1877. When it was erected, it was decided that a time capsule would be buried underneath it. Inside the capsule there is a selection of goodies of the day, including that morning's newspapers, hair pins, bibles, a box of cigars, pipes, a set of imperial weights, a baby's bottle, children's toys, a shilling razor, an hydraulic jack, some samples of the cable used in the erection of the needle, a 3-inch bronze model of the monument, a complete set of British coins, a rupee, a map of London and photographs of the twelve most beautiful English women of the day. There was also a portrait of Queen Victoria, who was sixty years old at the time.

⚜ COFFEE HOUSES: MEETING PLACES OF THE DAY ⚜

London's first coffee stall was opened in 1652, by a Greek man named Pasqua Roseé. He had worked as a servant for a British merchant in Smyrna, Turkey and developed a taste for the exotic Turkish drink. Roseé imported it to London, opened premises in Cornhill, and soon business was flourishing. Men travelled to consume the drink, said to taste like 'syrup of soot and essence of old shoes' – it

'The coffee house patriots', engraved by William Dickinson, 1781. (Library of Congress, LC-USZ62-20401)

has obviously improved considerably since then. The main functions of the coffee houses were for men to meet friends, think, smoke, debate, write and gossip. Gazettes, the precursors of newspapers, were distributed in the coffee houses, so that most functioned as reading rooms too.

Before they became popular, men would meet in taverns to do business. These were often unpleasant and rowdy places though, due to the ale consumed, and so were quite unproductive venues. Coffee, on the other hand, 'will prevent drowsiness and make one fit for business.' It was thought that the beverage might have medicinal properties, because in 1665, London doctor Gideon Harvey advised coffee was the drink to stop the plague spreading.

Not everyone thought coffee houses (or 'penny universities' as they had become known, because a dish of coffee cost a penny and came with unlimited refills) were fantastic places. For a start, women objected to the amount of time their husbands spent in them. In 1674, the Women's Petition Against Coffee was launched, stating in a pamphlet that coffee 'made men as unfruitful as the deserts whence that unhappy berry is said to be brought'. Despite earning substantial revenues from the sale of coffee, King Charles II tried to ban the establishments, condemning them as 'places where the disaffected met and spread scandalous reports concerning the conduct of his Majesty and his Ministers'. The outcry was such that he had to withdraw his proclamation.

From 1675, a thousand or so coffee houses sprung up as their popularity increased. One of these was Don Saltero's Coffee House, which opened in Lawrence Street before relocating to Chelsea's Cheyne Walk. It was run by James Salter, nicknamed 'Saltero' by Vice-Admiral Munded, who liked Spanish titles after spending time on the Spanish coast. Initially the coffee shop had a barber's section and, besides shaving his customers, Salter was also able to pull out their teeth, bleed them (a common medical practice of withdrawing blood to prevent illness, that was performed from antiquity until the late nineteenth century), play the violin and write them poetry; a man of many talents. The shop was famed for its many curiosities, which included 'a curious piece of metal found in the ruins of Troy, Pontius Pilate's wife's great-grandmother's hat, and a set of beads made from the bones of St Anthony of Padua.'

The best-known coffee houses began to attract a distinct clientele. In 1688, Edward Lloyd's Coffee House on Tower Street earned a reputation as the place to go for marine insurance. It later evolved into world-famous insurance market Lloyd's of London. In 1698, the owner of Jonathan's Coffee House in Exchange Alley began to issue a list of stock and commodity prices called 'The Course of the Exchange and other things', and so was the creation of the London Stock Exchange. Auction houses Sotheby's and Christie's also have their origins in coffee houses. Doctors used Batson's Coffee House in Cornhill as a consulting room. Chapter in Paul's Alley was the place to go for publishers and booksellers. Scientists Sir Isaac

Newton and Professor Halley frequented the Grecian on the Strand. Playwright Dryden and his contemporaries met at Will's in Russell Street in Covent Garden. Sometimes coffee houses were used for more formal, educational activities such as lectures, although they generally provided a base for clubs and societies. Slaughter's Coffee House in St Martin's Lane was established in 1692 and was a common meeting place for chess players, as well as Abraham de Moivre, who acted as the resident mathematician, providing advice on investments and financial matters.

There was even a floating coffee house, the *Folly of the Thames*, which was moored outside Somerset House, where people would dance until late at night. In its heyday, Queen Mary and some of her courtiers paid a visit out of curiosity, but as time went on the *Folly* began to attract a rather disreputable crowd. In time, it became so scandalous that it was closed, and the vessel was demolished and chopped up for use as firewood.

By 1700, over 500 coffee houses also sold tea and hot chocolate. Tavern owners were not particularly pleased about this, as it cut their sales of alcohol and it was bad news for the government too; they depended on a revenue stream from taxes on liquor sales. One of the first to offer tea was business-savvy Thomas Garraway, who owned a coffee house in Exchange Alley, Cornhill. He sold both liquid and dry tea to the public, at £6 and £10 per pound! He extolled its virtues as 'making the body active and lusty' and 'preserving perfect health until extreme old age'. It was finally closed in 1866.

Much earlier than that though, Samuel Pepys' diary makes reference to drinking tea for the first time on 25 September 1660, when he writes, '… afterwards I did send for a cup of tee (a China drink) of which I never had drank before.' He did not expound on what he thought of it though, but by 1750 tea had become the favoured drink of Britain's lower classes.

COSTERMONGERS – COUGH DROPS, COCOA AND SECOND-HAND CLOTHES

From the tenth century until the Victorian era, many street hawkers sold their wares in London's main market at Cheapside. The most successful were the 'costermongers' – the name comes from the 'costard' apple – and by the mid-1800s there were around 30,000 of them in London.

A journalist of the day, Henry Mayhew, recorded the array of goods for sale:

> … oysters, hot-eels, pea soup, fried fish, pies and puddings, sheep's trotters, pickled whelks, gingerbread, baked potatoes, crumpets, cough drops, cocoa, street-ices, ginger beer, cocoa and peppermint water as well as clothes, second-hand musical instruments, books and even birds' nests.

London central fruit and vegetable market. Engraving by Horace Jones, 1880. (Library of Congress, LC-DIG-ppmsca-12668)

There appears to have been quite a variety of goods on sale. Some costermongers specialised in procuring waste products to sell on, such as broken metal, bottles, bones and even dripping, broken candles and silver spoons. Most middle-class and working-class households depended on these street sellers, who had regular, predictable beats and made a fair living.

Each market district elected a 'Coster King' to safeguard their rights from competitors. Eventually, these Coster Kings became known as Pearly Kings. The founder of the organisation was Henry Croft, who grew up in an orphanage. At thirteen, he left to work as a road sweeper before being employed in a market. Here he worked alongside costermongers who decorated their suits with pearl buttons. Costermongers were caring folk and helped those who were even less fortunate than they were; homeless children, young chimneysweeps, disabled people who were forced to beg for food, and fellow traders who had fallen on hard times.

Henry was fascinated by this way of life and decided he would like to help those more unfortunate than himself, including the children at the orphanage where he had spent his early life. He realised that to collect enough money he needed to draw attention to himself, so started to collect buttons that he found and then sewed them onto his cap. Before long, he had covered his suit with buttons too. With so many of London's hospitals, workhouses and orphanages needing help, Henry called on the Costermongers to help him.

London's Pearly Kings and Queens collecting for charity. (Wikimedia Commons, photographer Garry Knight)

Many Coster Kings were members of friendly societies and in conjunction with hospitals, arranged fundraising events, fancy dress 'rag' parades and carnivals – hence the birth of the Pearly Kings and Queens. There were twenty-eight families, one for each of the London boroughs, one for the City of Westminster and one for the City of London. The Pearly motto is the very wise 'One Never Knows'.

DANCING WITH THE DEVIL
❧ IN BLEEDING HEART YARD ❧

The stirringly named Bleeding Heart Yard is on land once occupied by the gardens of the Bishop of Ely's palace, which Elizabeth I gave to her chancellor, Sir Christopher Hatton.

There is a legend that in the 1600s a grand ball took place at Hatton House, where glamorous Lady Hatton played the leading role. She was young, beautiful and wealthy and had no trouble in attracting attention from amorous male suitors. When the evening was in full swing, a man dressed all in black walked in, took Lady Hatton's hand and they began to dance around the room.

The mystery man was described as foreign, possibly Spanish, with a clawed right hand. Different versions of the tale come into play here. One is that the couple danced through the doors, into the garden and vanished. Then the skies opened, there was a crash of thunder and no one could find the couple. The guests apparently gossiped throughout the night, waiting to see if the couple would return – they did not. Other versions claim that Lady Hatton was simply spirited away.

The next morning, Lady Hatton's body was found in a cobbled courtyard behind the stable block of Hatton House. Her torso was ripped open and her limbs had been torn off, but her heart was still pumping blood out over the cobbles. It was supposed that the person with whom she was last seen dancing must have been the Devil. This is how the area came to be known as Bleeding Heart Yard.

DENTIST DISPLAYED HIS
❧ DEAD WIFE TO THE PUBLIC ❧

Eccentric dentist Martin van Butchell (1735–1814) kept his wife, Mary, on display in the window of his premises at 56 Mount Street after she died, in 1775. He had her embalmed by his teachers of surgery and anatomy, Dr William Hunter and Dr William Cruikshank, in the hope that the gruesome 'attraction' would draw more customers to his practice. Mary was placed in a glass-topped coffin and, although people flocked to see the body, Butchell also drew criticism for his

BY
HIS MAJESTY'S

Thus said sneaking Jack,   **ROYAL**   speaking like himself,
I'll be first; if I get my money,   I don't care who suffers

LETTERS PATENT,
MARTIN VAN BUTCHELL'S
NEW INVENTED
with caustic care——and old Phim
SPRING BANDS AND FASTENINGS
Sometimes in six days, and always ten—
the fistulæ in Ano.
FOR
THE APPAREL AND FURNITURE
July Sixth
OF
Licensed to deal in Perfumery, i. e.
HUMAN BEINGS
Hydrophobia cured in thirty days,
AND
BRUTE CREATURES
made of Milk and Honey,

Martin van Buttchell's advetisement. (© Walking London)

gruesome display. A rumour, possibly started by Butchell himself, claimed that a clause in their marriage certificate had provided income for him as long as Mary was 'above ground'.

Butchell began his career studying medicine and learning anatomy from the eminent Dr Hunter, but after having to treat one of his own teeth, he developed a particular interest in dentistry. He became a dentist in the 1760s, earning a reputation as one of the best in London. Butchell placed an advert in the *St James's Chronicle*: 'Real or Artificial Teeth from one to an entire set with superlative gold pivots or springs, also gums, sockets and palate formed, fitted, finished and fixed without drawing stumps, or causing pain.'

Butchell's eccentricity did not stop at keeping his dead wife handy and on view. He travelled around London with the bone of a Tahitian man attached to his wrist by a piece of string. He would not shave or trim his beard and published pamphlets about beard growth. He also made trusses, and was a specialist in treating anal fistulas. The unconventional dentist rode a white pony, which he painted with coloured spots, and summoned members of his family to him by individually modulated whistles. He was definitely something of an oddball.

When Butchell remarried, his second wife, Elizabeth, was more than a little miffed about her predecessor being kept permanently on show, and so the body was moved to the Royal College of Surgeons, only to be destroyed years later in a Second World War bombing raid.

DRANK VICTIMS' BLOOD
❧ THEN DISSOLVED THEM IN ACID ❧

On the surface, John Haigh was a respectable, charming, well-dressed middle-class man, but in the late 1940s he disposed of at least six victims in a way that led some to label him a vampire. He drank his victims' blood before he dissolved them in acid, because he believed that without a body there was no crime.

Haigh was raised in a fanatically religious household, and he claimed that his childhood was bleak and lonely; his only friends were his pets and the neighbour's dog. Haigh's parents belonged to an anticlerical sect, the Plymouth Brethren, and stories from the Bible were the only entertainment he had growing up. His parents forbade him from participating in sports.

In 1934, Haigh stopped attending his parents' church and married twenty-one-year-old Beatrice Hammer, whom he barely knew. His parents allowed the couple to live with them although the marriage was short-lived, ending when Haigh was arrested and convicted for fraud in October of the same year.

From that date, Haigh spent frequent spells in prison, mainly for fraudulent practices. While in jail he got the idea to target rich, older women, and after he was released he stayed with a family, developing a friendship with one of the daughters, Barbara. Shortly afterwards he rented a basement at 79 Gloucester Road, where he set up his 'workshop' to lure unsuspecting victims.

At a public house in Kensington, Haigh met a former employer, 'Mac' McSwan, who took Haigh to see his parents. During the reunion, they told Haigh of their recent investments and after socialising with Mac for several weeks, Haigh executed his new plan on 9 September 1944. In his diary, he wrote that he had a sudden need for blood, so he hit McSwan over the head before cutting his throat. Haigh said, 'I got a mug and took some blood from his neck, put it in the mug, and drank it.' He placed the body in a barrel, filled it with sulphuric acid and left his former employer and friend to dissolve. The next day the remains were little more than cold lumps, which Haigh disposed of down a drain. He convinced McSwan's parents that their son had gone away to avoid conscription and even sent them fake postcards from Scotland, pretending that they were from their son.

Haigh's main concern was to acquire the rest of the McSwan assets, but before he disposed of the other members of the family, he murdered a middle-aged woman from Hammersmith in a seemingly unconnected crime. The McSwans disappeared on 2 July 1945, suffering a fate similar to their son's and Haigh claimed to have drunk their blood before dissolving them in acid. He managed to have their mail forwarded to his address, which included Mr McSwan's pension, and forged a deed on a property owned by Mrs McSwan. In total, Haigh made a profit of nearly £2,000 by selling the property and amassed around £6,000 from securities and sales of possessions.

His next victims were fifty-two-year-old Dr Archibald Henderson and his wife, Rose, who was forty-one. This time Haigh shot them before drinking their blood and placing them in an acid bath, but his overconfidence led him to be careless and Mr Henderson's foot remained intact. This leftover body part did not bother Haigh, and he simply dumped all the remains in a yard. After managing to sell the Henderson's properties, he acquired around £8,000.

He then went on to meet the wealthy and elderly Mrs Olive Durand-Deacon, again disposing of her in acid. Interestingly, he reported her disappearance to the police and when they investigated, they found the trail led directly to Haigh. He was arrested and commented to the reception officer upon arrival at Lewes Prison, 'This is the result of doing six people, but not for personal gain'. He then confessed to everything. Haigh appeared to feel no remorse and he revealed his grisly escapades to the newspapers.

Even although the acid had destroyed a great deal of evidence, not everything was eliminated. The forensic team found small bones, dentures, Mr Henderson's foot and a gall bladder. During the court case, most of the psychologists who examined him agreed that, although Haigh suffered from mental health issues, he was not insane and had been perfectly aware of his actions. He possessed a talent for deception, having over the years also posed as a lawyer, engineer and doctor.

Haigh had no money to pay for his defence, so the *News of the World* newspaper made a deal with him and offered to pay for his counsel in return for providing them with an exclusive. The *Daily Mirror* was found in contempt of court for emphasising that Haigh was a vampire. The editor, Silvester Bolam, was sentenced to three months in prison and the paper had to pay £10,000 in court costs.

It took the jury just fifteen minutes to return a verdict of 'guilty'. The judge asked Haigh if he had anything to say for himself. Haigh cocked his head and said, 'Nothing at all'. The judge then sentenced him to death. Haigh finished his life story for the newspaper that had paid for his trial and on 6 August 1949, he was hanged at Wandsworth Prison.

❖ DRIVE ON THE RIGHT – IT'S THE LAW! ❖

There is one place in London where it is not only legal but also mandatory to drive on the right side of the road, and that is in Savoy Court in the Strand.

An Act of Parliament gave traffic, whether horse-drawn or mechanical, the right to drive on this side when entering Savoy Court from the Strand, because the Savoy Theatre is on the right-hand side. Taxis can deposit their fares directly outside the theatre without turning around in front of the Savoy Hotel, and when leaving they are then free to pick up a new fare from the hotel as they leave. It also means that the hotel entrance is never blocked.

The Savoy Hotel, which opened in 1889, was the first luxury hotel in Britain. It had all the mod cons of the day, including electric lights and lifts, en suite bedrooms, and hot and cold running water. Built by Richard D'Oyly Carte on land adjacent to his Savoy Theatre, the new hotel offered accommodation for the many tourists – especially Americans – who travelled to London to see the Savoy Operas. Additionally the hotel's restaurants, bars, lounges, private dining rooms and banqueting suites offered choices for Londoners who wanted to enjoy themselves in plush surroundings. Cesar Ritz, later to become world famous for his Ritz hotels, opened the main restaurant and installed August Escoffier, 'king of chefs and chef of kings', in the Savoy kitchen.

Egyptian prince, Fahmy Bey, was shot dead at the Savoy Hotel in 1923 by his French wife, Marguerite. She was acquitted of murder after it was revealed that her husband had treated her cruelly throughout their six-month marriage, and had threatened to kill her.

During the Second World War, the managing director, Hugh Wontner, and staff had to cope with bomb damage, food rationing, shortage of manpower and a serious decline in the number of foreign visitors. After the Americans joined the war, business picked up again as the Savoy Hotel became a favourite visiting place for American officers, diplomats and journalists. Winston Churchill often took his cabinet to lunch at the hotel and regular visitors to

Savoy Court in the 1920s. (© Savoy Hotel)

Vintage envelope. (© Savoy Hotel)

the Grill Room were Lord Mountbatten and Charles de Gaulle. The hotel's air-raid shelters were described as London's smartest. Wontner cooperated fully with the government's wartime restrictions and helped to draw up an order imposing a five-shilling limit on the price of a restaurant meal (around £10 in today's money).

Another curiosity near to the Savoy Hotel is Carting Lane. Sewer gases originally illuminated the bulb of a Webb sewer gas lamp, which is still there today. These lamps were used for two reasons: firstly to burn off the smells and germs from London's sewer system, and secondly as a low cost way to keep London lit up at night. Until the 1950s, the bowel movements of Savoy guests helped to light the street outside, making it a successful early (though perhaps strange) form of recycling.

Methane was collected by a small dome in the roof of the sewer, with the gas then diverted into the lamp on the street above. The lamp remained lit for twenty-four hours, seven days a week and powered at least partly by an almost unlimited amount of waste from guests staying at the hotel, which is why the street used to be called the rather rude 'Farting Lane'.

Laurence Olivier and Marilyn Monroe at the Savoy in 1956. (© Savoy Hotel)

Interestingly, the effluence from the sewers was not actually concentrated enough to give full power to the lamps and instead the lamps were 'dual powered' by ordinary town gas supplies, which heated the filament up to around 700 degrees Fahrenheit. This heat then drew the methane and other gases from the sewer system, in turn ventilating up to three quarters of a mile of pipe. The current lamp now runs on standard gas.

❧ DUCHESS OF KINGSTON, BIGAMIST AND BEAUTY ❧

Elizabeth Chudleigh, who became the Duchess of Kingston, was born in 1720. She was the only daughter of Thomas Chudleigh, who at the time of his death, when Elizabeth was five, was administrator to the Royal Hospital in Chelsea. Although they were an aristocratic family, they did not have a lot of money.

When Elizabeth was twenty-two, her mother Henriette managed to get William Pulteney (1st Earl of Bath), who had been one of her husband's friends, to help Elizabeth secure the position of maid of honour to Augusta, Princess of Wales.

Soon Elizabeth became infamous for her succession of affairs with important and influential men, including King George II. In 1744, she married a Royal Navy officer, Augustus Hervey, who became 3rd Earl of Bristol. They hid the fact that they were married so that she could retain her position with the Princess of Wales, but it soon became apparent it was not a happy marriage and they went their separate ways.

Elizabeth had a black servant called Sambo, who she raised from the age of five. She dressed him in fine clothes and took him on regular visits to the theatre, where they sat together in her box. During this time, there was a trend for wealthy families to employ young black boys as pages; it was a sign of how sophisticated the family was and that they were important enough to have colonial connections. This dated back to the seventeenth century, when Oliver Cromwell acquired West Indian colonies, including Jamaica and Barbados. Many local children were taken from their families and brought to London as status symbols for the aristocracy.

Sambo lived quite a luxurious life with the Duchess until he was about eighteen or nineteen, when he started to meet undesirable types. Elizabeth would not tolerate such behaviour and sent him back to the West Indies.

She was a colourful character, rather unrefined and infamous for notorious exploits. At the Ranelagh May Ball in 1749, she appeared as Iphigenia from Greek legend and her wispy costume was so transparent that one guest remarked she appeared 'so naked, the high priest might easily inspect the entrails of the victim.'

She became the mistress of Evelyn Pierrepont, 2nd Duke of Kingston. Later they married and lived in Kingston House, a Palladian mansion in Westminster.

Meanwhile, Hervey became heir to the Earldom of Bristol. When the 2nd Earl of Bristol fell ill in 1759, Elizabeth, always with an eye on how to make more money, forged an entry in the church register, hoping to support a later claim as Countess, although marriage to the Duke of Kingston was a better prospect. Hervey also wished to make another marriage, so the pair decided to conceal evidence of their wedding.

Kingston died in 1773. If she remained a widow, Elizabeth was entitled to his estate revenues and all of his personal effects, but the Duke's will was disputed by his disinherited nephew, Evelyn Medows, who brought a case of bigamy against her.

The trial took place in 1776 in front of the House of Lords and lasted for a period of five days. After hearing the evidence, all 119 Lords took it in turn to declare their verdict. Each spoke the word 'guilty'. The Duchess was charged and convicted of bigamy, although she escaped punishment by fleeing to Europe.

She retained a substantial fortune left to her by the Duke of Kingston and during the last two years of her life, she lived in France and Russia, for a time at the court of Catherine the Great. She died suddenly on 26 August 1788.

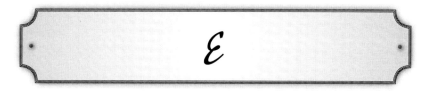

$\mathcal{E}$

❖ EEL PIE ISLAND ❖

The only way to get to the privately owned Eel Pie Island on the Thames at Twickenham is by footbridge or boat. The traffic-free island used to be called Twickenham Ait and before that The Parish Ait. It has about fifty houses, some small businesses and artist studios with nature reserves at either end, though they are not accessible to the public.

In the 1960s, the island was a major jazz and blues venue. The Eel Pie Island Hotel once stood here, though sadly it is no longer. Charles Dickens described the hotel as a 'place to dance to the music of the locomotive band', while in the 1920s it was a popular venue for tea dances. The hotel also played host to some of the most influential British performers of traditional jazz, including Ken Colyer, Acker Bilk and Chris Barber. Many years before this, Henry VIII was rumoured to pop by the island to fill his stomach with eel pies before entertaining his mistresses.

The Eel Pie Studios, or Oceanic Studios, located at The Boathouse on the mainland nearby, was formerly owned by Pete Townshend and was the venue for several significant pop and rock recordings. Townshend's publishing company, Eel Pie Publishing, is also named after the ait.

Eel Pie Island. (Wikimedia Commons, photographer 'Motmit')

⚜ ELEPHANT MAN: JOSEPH MERRICK ⚜

Joseph Carey Merrick (1862–1890), sometimes referred to as John Merrick, was exhibited as a human curiosity known as the Elephant Man. He was well known in London society after he went to live at the London Hospital. Merrick had developed abnormally during the first few years of his life with thick, lumpy skin, enlarged lips, arms and feet, and a bony growth on his forehead.

In 1884, Merrick contacted a showman named Sam Torr and proposed that he should exhibit him. It was arranged for a group of men to manage Merrick, whom they nicknamed the Elephant Man. Merrick travelled to London to be shown in a shop window at 259 Whitechapel Road, as a curiosity to entice people to come in to see a 'freak show'. The shop, rented by showman Tom Norman, was directly across the street from the London Hospital. A surgeon named Frederick Treves saw Merrick and took him to be examined and photographed. Soon after Merrick's visits to the hospital, the police closed the shop and Merrick's managers sent him to tour in Europe.

In Belgium, Merrick was robbed by his road manager and abandoned in Brussels. He eventually made his way back to London. Unable to communicate, the police found he had Frederick Treves' card on him. Treves came and took Merrick back to the London Hospital.

Although his condition was incurable, Merrick was allowed to stay at the hospital for the remainder of his life. Treves visited him daily and they developed quite a close friendship. Merrick also received visits from wealthy ladies and gentlemen of London society, including Alexandra, Princess of Wales.

Merrick died on 11 April 1890, aged twenty-seven. The official cause of death was asphyxia, although Treves, who dissected the body, said that Merrick had died of a dislocated neck. He believed that Merrick, who slept sitting up because of the weight of his head, had been attempting to sleep lying down, to 'be like other people'.

The exact cause of Merrick's deformities is unclear. It was initially thought that he suffered from Elephantiasis, a parasitic infection characterised by the thickening and enlargement of skin and tissue, akin to that of an elephant. Then, in 2001, some scientists suggested that Merrick had suffered from a rare disease called Proteus syndrome, a congenital disorder that causes skin overgrowth and abnormal bone development. Other experts questioned the diagnosis, saying that the way his disease manifested was not typical of that condition. Tests continue on his skeleton and it is hoped that eventually research will finally prove conclusive.

⁂ FIELD OF THE FORTY FOOTSTEPS ⁂

Two brothers in the Duke of Monmouth's rebellion engaged in a duel over a girl. Legend has it that each step they took during the duel killed the grass and it never grew back. The only building here on the meadowlands at the time was Montague House, home of the 1st Duke of Montagu, and now part of the British Museum. In the late eighteenth century, the poet Robert Southey went in search of the 'Brothers' Steps' and found them:

> … about three-quarters of a mile of [*sic*] Montagu House, and about five hundred yards east of Tottenham Court Road. They are of the size of a large human foot, about three inches deep, and lie nearly from north-east to south-west … the place where one or both

British Museum. (© VisitBritain / britainonview)

of the brothers are supposed to have fallen is still bare grass. [We also saw] the bank where (the tradition is) the wretched woman sat to see the combat.

⚜ FISHY BUSINESS AND ROMAN RUINS ⚜

Billingsgate, once known as Blynesgate and Byllynsgate, was originally a general market selling iron, corn, wine, coal, salt, pottery, fish and other goods. It did not become associated exclusively with the fish trade until the sixteenth century, and in 1699, a Parliamentary Act made it 'a free and open market for all sorts of fish whatsoever'. The only exception to this was the sale of eels, which was restricted to Dutch fishermen whose boats were moored in the Thames, because they had helped feed the people of London during the Great Fire.

Until the mid-nineteenth century, stalls and sheds around the 'hythe' or dock at Billingsgate were packed with fish and seafood for sale. As the amount of fish handled increased, a purpose-built market became essential. In 1850, the first Billingsgate Market building was constructed on Lower Thames Street. The building is still there and the link to its history is apparent by the fishy weathervanes on top of the building and other fish motifs on the walls.

Billingsgate Market. (Engraving published as Plate 9 of Microcosm of London 1808, Wikimedia Commons)

The coarse language of London fishmongers made 'Billingsgate' a byword for crude or vulgar language. One of its earliest uses is in a 1577 chronicle by Raphael Holinshed, where the writer refers to the foul tongues of Billingsgate. The 'wives' of Billingsgate used to carry baskets of fish on their heads. These women called fish 'fags', smoked tobacco, drank gin and were known for their colourful language.

In Peter Ackroyd's book, *London: The Biography*, he describes the market as having 'an atmosphere of reeking fish, with fish-scales underfoot and a shallow lake of mud all round.'

Four-hundred-year-old bylaws still dictate that stock cannot be moved before 5 a.m., despite traders arriving for work by 2 a.m. Until recently, only registered porters were allowed to move fish around the market, a role dating back at least to Henry VIII and officially recognised by the Corporation of London in 1632. However, in 2012 there was a difference of opinion between modernists, who disagreed with practices like porters earning £700 for working seventeen hours per week, and traditionalists, who wanted things to remain as they always had. The modernists won and the role of the porters has ceased.

The market can claim employees such as George Orwell, who worked at Billingsgate in the 1930s, and the Kray twins, who worked there in the 1950s. Hidden beneath an office building in Lower Thames Street, just a short distance from the former Billingsgate Fish Market, are the remains of some of London's

Billingsgate Fish Market. (Wikimedia Commons, photographer Jorge Ryan)

best preserved Roman ruins in the form of a house and baths complex. Workers building the New Coal Exchange in 1848 discovered the remains of the buildings. This was demolished in the 1960s and the current office building constructed in its place in the 1970s. The ruins are in the basement.

Though the house dates back to the 2nd century AD, it is believed that the baths were added the following century and they are thought to be located in the house's courtyard. The buildings, both of which feature an underfloor heating system called a hypocaust, are noted for the fact that they remained in use until the early 5th century AD, when much of what had been Roman Londinium was already in decline.

Visitors to the baths would first have visited the cold room (frigidarium), before moving on to the warm room (tepidarium), and then to the hot room (caldarium) which were heated by the hypocaust. There they would remove dirt and oils from their skin using curved metal scrapers called strigils, before going back to the cold room where they probably went into a plunge pool or splashed themselves with cold water. The site includes two furnaces, one at the house and another at the baths, used for heating the under floor space. It is likely that the owners were wealthy, as both buildings were stone built.

Objects found in the premises include a hoard of bronze coins minted after 395 AD and a bronze brooch that is believed to date after 450 AD, when the bathhouse may already have been in ruins.

In 1982, the market relocated to the Isle of Dogs in Docklands. Most fish sold at the market now arrives there by road, from ports as far afield as Aberdeen and Cornwall.

❧ FOUNDLING HOSPITAL ❧

Captain Thomas Coram (1668–1751) was a successful shipwright who was horrified by the sight of deserted and dying children on London's streets. He spent seventeen years campaigning for the establishment of the Foundling Hospital.

It eventually opened in Guilford Street in 1741, to look after the abandoned babies of unmarried mothers. On admittance, children were baptised and given a new name, and until the end of the eighteenth century, mothers left a personal item as a token that could be used to identify the child if she made a request to claim them later. The tokens are displayed within the Foundling Hospital Collection.

Unfortunately, arguments over which children were allocated the limited spaces provoked riots, and the hospital could not single out the children of mothers who were not harlots, as had been originally intended. In 1756, the government gave the hospital money to expand capacity on the condition that it accepted *all* children under two months old. Despairing mothers paid 'businessmen' to give their unwanted babies to the State, but many were lost or dead on arrival.

Three quarters of the 15,000 babies that reached the hospital died before the government ended its support in 1760.

The hospital moved to Berkhamstead in 1926, when the governors came to the decision that living in central London was not good for the health of the children. The hospital has since closed down. Whilst the Foundling Hospital's doors were open, it cared for over 25,000 children. Some of the architecture of the building in Guilford Street still survives, including the gateway and lodges where mothers would leave their babies in a basket.

⅜ FREEDOM OF THE CITY OF LONDON ⅜

The granting of the Freedom of the City is one of London's oldest surviving traditions, dating back to the thirteenth century. A 'freeman' was someone who was not the property of a feudal lord and who enjoyed privileges including the right to earn money and own land, essential for anybody who wanted to work as a tradesman.

It meant that they could carry out their trade, or craft, as a member of one of the venerable City of London Livery Companies, which was akin to a medieval trade union to regulate prices, quality and standards. It looked after their members; they were the only people to be given trading rights in the richest part of the kingdom. The fee was a slight deterrent, as it was considerably higher than the small fee of £25–30 charged today. The mayor and the City expected the guild to maintain excellent quality in the services provided – vintners were not allowed to give customers poor wine, and bakers could not sell stale bread.

Membership provided other privileges, including the right to herd sheep over London Bridge, to carry a drawn sword in the City, to avoid being press-ganged, to be married in St Paul's Cathedral, to be drunk and disorderly without being arrested, and, if their children were orphaned, to have them educated free at the Freeman's School in Kent. Freemen could also direct a gaggle of geese down Cheapside according to *The Freedom of the City of London*, which was a book of traditional ceremonies and privileges first presented in 1237.

Today the Freedom is largely symbolic and represents a slice of London's history.

FROM FORTUNE-TELLER TO ⅜ BEAUTICIAN AND BLACKMAILER ⅜

Wearing make-up was frowned upon in Victorian times and any woman suspected of using cosmetics was excluded from polite society. In fact, make-up was such a taboo that a man could divorce his wife for using it. Queen Victoria was horrified at the growing popularity of cosmetics; it was a common view that only actresses and prostitutes should prettify themselves in such a way. General opinion was that females could maintain their beauty with the vigorous use of soap and water, plenty of fresh air, and – as one Victorian doctor advised – 'not too much dancing' as it gave an undignified flush to the cheeks.

However, some forward-thinking Victorian women ignored the rule and exclaimed 'thank goodness' for Sarah Rachel Russell (also Leverson or Levison). Known as 'Madame Rachel', she opened a beauty salon in New Bond Street with the promise of 'everlasting youth' to her customers.

Some reports say Russell was born around 1806, others claim 1820, which seems to be nearer the mark. She was originally a fortune-teller in London's East End before changing her career to beauty, and soon she was earning money from wealthy women eager to believe her claims of 'miraculous' treatments. Russell told everybody she was much older than she was in order to emphasise how wonderful her skin products were, although these only contained ingredients like Fuller's earth and the harmful hydrochloric acid. Her products were expensive, with the cheapest costing around 10 shillings (approximately £30 in today's money) and the most expensive costing 10–20 guineas (around £1,700) for a bottle of 'rejuvenating Jordan Water'.

Russell placed the following advertisement in the *Morning Post* in 1859: 'Beautiful women, Madame Rachel begs to inform her lady patronesses, the nobility and aristocracy generally, that she has opened her annual subscription list for the supply of her Costly Arabian Preparations for the restoration and preservation of female loveliness.'

She also published a pamphlet called 'Beautiful Forever' in which she wrote that almost all cosmetics (except her own) were composed of 'deadly leads', but that her preparations were made from the purest, rarest and most fragrant products of the East.

Madame Rachel declared war on wrinkles and claimed that they would be banished forever if one purchased her 'fabulous' preparations. One of her most popular treatments was 'enamelling', in which she said she could make any woman's face white and porcelain smooth; the trend of the day. The treatment cost around 20 guineas, even though all she did was fill in wrinkles with white paste before finishing off with rouge and powder. *Punch* magazine stated that anyone thus enhanced would resemble nothing more than 'a white sepulchre'. However, Madame Rachel continued to promote herself by stating that 'all other persons presuming to style themselves enamellers commit a gross fraud on the public at large'. She even falsely claimed to be 'purveyor to Her Majesty the Queen'.

One of her most expensive beauty treatments was 'The Royal Arabian Toilet of Beauty as arranged by Madame Rachel for the Sultana of Turkey', which cost around 1,000 guineas. The price was no deterrent and women flocked to her shop for the treatment.

Russell also swore by her 'magnetic rock water dew' from the 'sands of the Sahara'. Eventually this was exposed as ordinary water mixed with bran, although some of the more gullible women of the day found her claims irresistible. Women then, as now, pursued beauty at any price, often taking risks with harmful cosmetics. The only difference was that they did so then in secret, making it easier for Madame Rachel to rip them off financially and threaten them with blackmail. Too ashamed of their actions, they did not dare tell their husbands what had happened.

Her income was also boosted by wealthy men who paid to look through peepholes at her clients in their Arabian baths, although some of the women behaved just as badly and used the premises to conduct affairs. One paid Madame Rachel a generous sum in the hope of being supplied with a husband.

Of course, business did not continue to run smoothly, and Madame Rachel ended up in prison for ten years for cheating one of her customers, a wealthy widow called Mary Borrodaile. (Not that it ruined her business for long, because the increased publicity led to further riches.) Madame Rachel had told the woman that Lord Ranelagh, whom Mary had met accidentally in the shop one day, was enamoured with her. She suggested that Mary start an extensive – and expensive – beauty regime. To encourage Mary even more, she herself wrote letters purportedly from Lord Ranelagh and passed them on to her. Mary spent thousands on 'improving herself' until some of her friends realised it was a con and charges were filed.

Russell was so shocked at the severity of the sentence that she fainted. The *Illustrated London News* found her plight somewhat pathetic: 'Surely the court should have been full of perfume, and enamel, and chignons … Have the plastered and dyed and painted over all forsaken their Jewess?' Sergeant Ballentine, who led the prosecution, declared her to be 'one of the most filthy and dangerous moral pests that have existed in my time.' After she was released from prison, Russell re-established herself near Portman Square. However, in 1878, she was arrested again for fraud and she later died in jail.

G

⚜ GHOSTS OF THE TOWER OF LONDON ⚜

Beheadings, murders, torture and hangings – all manner of grisly things happened in the Tower of London, so it is hardly surprising that a phantom or two lingers within its walls. In the past 900 years, the building has developed the reputation of being one of the most haunted places in Britain.

One of the first sightings was that of Thomas A. Becket. During construction on the Inner Curtain Wall, Thomas's shade appeared, apparently unhappy about the work being carried out. The story goes that he reduced the wall to rubble with a strike of his cross. Henry III's grandfather was responsible for Becket's death, so Henry III wasted no time in building a chapel in the Tower, naming it for the archbishop. It must have pleased Becket, because there were no further interruptions during the construction of the wall. The St Thomas Tower is also known as Traitors' Gate, because it was through here that condemned prisoners accused of treason arrived from Westminster.

The Tower of London. (© VisitLondon / britainonview)

The 'Bloody Tower' was the scene of the infamous disappearance of the two young princes: twelve-year-old Edward V and ten-year-old Richard, Duke of York, who were the sons of King Edward IV. No one knows exactly what happened to the brothers, but it is thought that they were murdered upon their uncle's instructions. The Duke of Gloucester was determined to wear the crown and did not want anyone to get in his way. By July 1483, they were declared illegitimate and the Duke was crowned King Richard III. In 1485, he was killed at the Battle of Bosworth. The victor, Henry Tudor, crowned King Henry VII, is also considered a suspect in their disappearance. He married the princes' sister, Elizabeth of York, strengthening his claim to the throne, which could have been jeopardised if the boys had survived.

Fifteenth-century guards, who were passing the Bloody Tower one night, saw the shadows of two small figures gliding down the stairs, still dressed in the white nightshirts they were wearing when they disappeared. They stopped and stood hand-in-hand, before fading back into the wall. These two figures are thought to be the ghosts of the two princes. In the 1600s, workers discovered a chest containing children's skeletons, and, believing they were the remains of the princes, they were given a royal burial. Today they are among the most poignant ghosts in the Tower of London.

The most persistent ghost must be that of Queen Anne Boleyn. When King Henry VIII learned that the new baby was a boy and stillborn, he accused her of infidelity. She was taken to Tower Green and beheaded on 19 May 1536. Queen Anne's shade has been seen near the Queen's House, close to the site where she was executed, and has on occasion led a ghostly procession down the aisle of the Chapel Royal of St Peter ad Vincula. She is buried under the altar and it is said that her headless body has been seen walking the corridors of the Tower.

Explorer and adventurer Sir Walter Raleigh is famed for placing his cloak on the mud so that Queen Elizabeth I could cross the road without getting her shoes dirty. He lived quite comfortably compared to other prisoners of the Bloody Tower and was assigned two rooms on the second floor, where he lived for thirteen years (they are still furnished now as they were then). Raleigh was freed to look for the lost city of El Dorado, but when he failed to find it, he was sent back to prison. Although the explorer was executed in Old Palace Yard at Westminster, visitors have reported seeing his ghost looking exactly as he appears in the portrait hanging in the Bloody Tower.

The most grisly execution of all is that of the seventy-year-old Countess of Salisbury, last of the Plantagenets. King Henry VIII had her executed for political reasons. The feisty Countess refused to put her head on the block and when her executioner chased her, she ran, with him pursuing her with his axe in hand, hacking at her until she was dead. Her ghost is said to relive this gruesome act and the shadow of a great axe has been seen falling across the site of her execution.

Something so scary that dogs will not enter the ancient building haunts the Salt Tower. Ever since one of the Yeoman Warders was almost throttled by an unseen force, they will not go near the area after nightfall. In 1864, a soldier whose post was guarding the Queen's House at the Tower, saw an apparition so real that he ignored soldiers' challenges and charged the intruder with his bayonet, only to travel straight through the figure. He was found unconscious on the spot and was court-martialled for neglecting his duty. Luckily, there were two witnesses to corroborate his story and the soldier was eventually acquitted.

Helmet of Henry VIII, on display at the Tower of London and dating to 1515. (© Gary Ombler Royal Armouries Historic Royal Palaces)

Lady Jane Grey, the granddaughter of King Henry VIII's younger sister, Mary and Louis XII of France, also suffered a sad fate at the Tower. After Edward VI died in 1553, Lady Jane became Queen of England. She was only sixteen years of age; a clever girl who not only excelled in needlework and music, but could also speak Latin, Greek, French and Italian. Jane was not happy when she heard the news that she was to be crowned, and for a time refused to accept the position. Eventually, she was persuaded to take the role by her father and husband.

When the public announcement was made that she was Queen, her subjects were not happy either; they had expected Mary to become the next monarch. A vintner's boy was so displeased that he voiced his opinions publicly, which he no doubt regretted the next day when he had his ears nailed to the pillory, and then cut off.

Mary desperately wanted to be Queen and her supporters helped to overthrow Jane. The Duke of Suffolk had to tell Jane that she was no longer going to be crowned, to which she replied that she had not wanted the title anyway and had accepted only out of obedience to his wishes. Her nine days' reign was over.

Concerned that there might be further problems, Queen Mary and her court decided to commit the Duke of Suffolk and Lady Jane to the Tower. The Duke, thanks to his wife, procured a pardon, but Lady Jane and her husband, Lord Dudley, were tried and sentenced to death for treason. The sentence was not immediately carried out and the Queen seemed to want to spare their lives. Unfortunately, owing to the general dislike of her marriage to Philip of Spain, Sir Thomas Wyatt

The Tower of London. (© VisitBritain / Pavel Libera)

raised a rebellion along with the Duke of Suffolk and his brothers. After it had been controlled, Queen Mary was persuaded that it was unsafe to spare the lives of Lady Jane and her husband any longer.

Both Jane and her husband were beheaded at Tower Hill. Her ghost was last seen by two Guardsmen on 12 February 1957, the 403rd anniversary of her execution. She was described as a 'white shape forming itself on the battlements'. Her husband, Guildford Dudley, has been seen weeping in Beauchamp Tower.

Catherine Howard, fifth wife of Henry VIII, escaped from her room in the Tower of London after being held captive in her private chambers. She ran down the hallway screaming for help and mercy, but was dragged back to her rooms. She was told that her husband had left for Oatland Palace in Surrey, where he would stay until after her execution, which was to be the next day. Well, it was never a good bet to marry King Henry VIII, although he had showered her with jewels and genuinely cared for his 'Rose without a Thorn', until he discovered she had been unfaithful to him with Thomas Culpepper, who was also beheaded. Catherine's ghost has been seen running down the hallway screaming in terror.

Major General Geoffrey Field was Governor of the Tower of London from 1994 to 2006, and he lived in the Queen's House on Tower Green with his family. He said:

> Soon after we arrived in 1994, my wife Janice was making up the bed in the Lennox room when she felt a violent push in her back which propelled her right out of the room. No one had warned us that the house was haunted but we then discovered that every resident has experienced something strange in that room. The story goes that the ghost is that of Arabella Stuart, a cousin of James I, who was imprisoned and then possibly murdered in that bedroom. Several women who slept there since have reported waking in terror in the middle of the night feeling they were being strangled, so just in case, we made it a house rule not to give unaccompanied female guests the Lennox room.

There is no doubt dark deeds tar the history of the Tower.

❧ GIN JOINTS ❧

In the 1730s, over 6,000 houses in London sold gin to the public. By the 1750s, Londoners were knocking back an incredible 11 million gallons of gin a year.

Gin was originally touted as medicinal, believed to cure gout and indigestion, but its prime appeal for the poor was that it was a cheap and strong drink, and offered a quick release from the misery of everyday life. Some workers received gin as part of their wages, but other people would do anything to procure it – in the mid-1700s a coachman pawned his wife for a quart bottle, and a cattle drover sold his eleven-year-old daughter to a trader for a gallon of gin. Gin joints in eighteenth-century London allowed women to drink alongside men for the first time and it was suggested that this led to child neglect and prostitution, coining the term 'Mother's ruin'. In 1734, a woman named Judith Dufour collected her two-year-old child from the workhouse, strangled him, dumped the body in a ditch and sold his new clothes for 1*s* and 4*d* to buy gin.

William Hogarth depicted the craze in his engraving 'Gin Lane', which showed Bloomsbury scenes of a semi-naked, drunk woman covered in syphilitic sores, who does not realise that her baby is about to fall to its death down a set of stairs. The novelist Henry Fielding said that there would soon be 'few of the common people left to drink it' if the situation continued. In fact, during that time, one in eight Londoners drank themselves to death.

As the problem escalated, the government was forced to take action. In 1736, the Gin Act was passed making it illegal to buy gin in small quantities, leading to a black market that resulted in even more devastating effects. Gin, which went by colourful names such as 'Ladies Delight' and 'Cuckold's Comfort', was often poisonous and sometimes ingredients like sulphuric acid were used in the brewing process. It did not help that water was unsafe to drink at the time and sweetened gin was the preferred alternative.

Then the Gin Act of 1751 was passed. This was more successful. It lowered the licence fee and forced distillers to sell only to licensed retailers trading from respectable premises. A change in the economy also helped turn the tide. A series of bad harvests forced grain prices up, making land owners less dependent on income from gin production. Food prices rose and wages went down, so the poor were less able to afford to buy gin.

In 1830, the Duke of Wellington's administration passed the Sale of Beer Act, which removed all taxes on beer and permitted anyone to open a beer shop on payment of a two-guinea fee. This Bill virtually ended gin smuggling. By the end of 1830, there were 24,000 beer shops in England and Wales.

Viaduct Tavern in Newgate Street (EC1) opened in 1869, the same year as the nearby Holborn Viaduct, the world's first flyover, was opened by Queen Victoria. It is a rare example of the Victorian gin palace. An imposing, wide frontage hides a small interior, a mass of gilt mirrors, engraved glass and snugs, a copper ceiling and ornate columns.

⚜ GREAT FIRE OF LONDON ⚜

The Great Fire of London was a momentous disaster in the city's history. It started in the early hours of 2 September 1666 and lasted just under five days. In this time, it destroyed around a third of London and made about 100,000 people homeless.

The fire started in Thomas Farriner's bakery on Pudding Lane, which got its name from the 'pudding' or offal that fell from butchers' carts as they trundled to the waste barges on the Thames. Farriner was the King's baker. It is unlikely that the cause of the fire will ever be known, but it spread rapidly because London was bone dry after a long, hot summer and the area around Pudding Lane was packed with warehouses containing highly flammable materials like timber, rope and oil.

Map of old London, 1666. The white part represents the area affected by the fire. (Wikimedia Commons)

Frenchman Robert Hubert later confessed to starting the Great Fire and was hanged, but it turned out that he was not in London when the fire started. The Earl of Clarendon commented that, 'Neither the judges, nor any present at the trial did believe him guilty; but that he was a poor distracted wretch, weary of his life, and chose to part with it.'

The fire spread quickly and most Londoners concentrated on escaping rather than fighting the fire. They rescued as many of their belongings as they could carry and fled. Thomas Farriner and his family climbed out of an upstairs window and onto their neighbour's roof to escape the fire in their bakery, but the maid was too timid to follow suit and died in the fire.

Some Londoners fled to the river and tried to load their goods onto boats. Other residents went to the fields outside London where they stayed for several days, sheltering in tents. There was no fire brigade in 1666, so it was up to the local residents and soldiers to fight the fire. They used buckets of water, water squirts and fire hooks. The best way to stop the fire was to pull down houses with hooks to make gaps or 'fire breaks', although this was difficult because the wind forced the fire across any gaps created. Mayor Sir Thomas Bludworth complained, 'The fire overtakes us faster than we can do it.' He had changed his tune, as originally he was quite unconcerned about the damage the fire might do and had commented, 'A woman could piss it out'.

A quicker way of demolishing houses was to blow them up with gunpowder, but this technique was not used until the third day of the fire. Fire Posts, each staffed by 130 men, were set up around the city to fight the blaze, but the damage caused by the fire was immense. Four hundred and thirty-six acres of London were destroyed, including 13,200 houses and eighty-seven out of 109 churches. Some locations smouldered for months. St Paul's Cathedral was ruined, as was the Guildhall and fifty-two livery company halls. Oddly, fewer than ten deaths were recorded as a direct result of the fire, although Samuel Pepys noted that many pigeons lost their lives because they refused to leave their nests, subsequently their wing feathers were burned and they plummeted into the fire.

He also recorded in his diary: 'I saw a fire as one entire arch of fire above a mile long: it made me weep to see it. The churches, houses are all on fire and flaming at once, and a horrid noise the flames made and the cracking of the houses.' Pepys dug a pit in which to bury 'a parmazan cheese as well as my wine and some other things', and also recorded the demolishing of houses with gunpowder: 'Blowing up houses … stopped the fire when it was done, bringing down the houses in the same places they stood, and then it was easy to quench what little fire was in it.'

On the Wednesday morning, the fire had reached Middle Temple and Fetter Lane. Workers pulled down more buildings to widen the break. The wind slackened and changed direction, turning south and blowing the fire onto itself and towards the river. In the north, it was being checked at Smithfield and Holborn Bridge and the Mayor was directing demolition in Cripplegate. By dawn on Thursday, the fire was out.

It took nearly fifty years to rebuild the ruined city and new regulations came into being to prevent such a disaster happening again – houses had to be faced in brick instead of wood; some streets were widened; pavements and new sewers were laid. The results were noticeable: '[London] is not only the finest, but the most healthy city in the world,' said one proud Londoner. It was a big improvement for some parts of the city, where raw sewage had flowed in gutters straight into the Thames.

In 1979, archaeologists excavated the remains of a burnt-out shop on Pudding Lane, which was close to the bakery where the fire had started. They found the charred remnants of twenty barrels of pitch (tar) in the cellar. Among the burnt objects from the shop, they also found melted pieces of pottery, which showed that the temperature of the fire was as high as 1,700 degrees Celsius.

Contrary to some beliefs, the Great Fire did not stop the Great Plague of 1665, as the plague affected a much larger area than the part destroyed in the fire.

The Monument to the Great Fire of London stands at the junction of Monument Street and Fish Street Hill in the City. It was built between 1671 and 1677. The 202ft-tall landmark is said to have been placed so precisely that if it should ever be tipped over it will point to the exact spot where this great blaze began.

⁂ GROOM OF THE STOOL ⁂

The sanitary needs of Tudor courtiers at Hampton Court Palace were met in a variety of ways. The lodgings of the senior members of the court, such as those in Base Court, had their own 'garderobe' shafts. Lower-ranking members of the court used the 'common jakes' in the south-west corner of the palace, later known as the Great House of Easement, where lavatories drained via the moat into the river. Fourteen people could be seated there simultaneously.

The grandest people used a 'close stool', which was a padded seat placed over a chamber pot. The Groom of the Stool, with access to the bedchamber, closet and close stool room, was the king's most intimate and, therefore, most powerful servant. Among other duties, 'he preside[d] over the office of royal excretion.' The close stool used by William III remains in the King's Apartments at Hampton Court Palace and is on view today. His Groom of the Stool was Hans Willem Bentinck, Earl of Portland.

In the early years of Henry VIII's reign, the title was awarded to minions of the King, who were court companions that spent time with him in the 'Privy' chamber. These were the sons of noblemen or important members of the gentry. In time, they came to act as personal secretaries to the King, carrying out a variety of administrative tasks within his private rooms. The position was an especially prized one, as it allowed unobstructed access to the King's attention. Despite being his official lavatory assistant, the Groom of the Stool had a high social standing.

Deaf and half-blind King George II got up early one morning in October 1760 in Kensington Palace, drank a cup of hot chocolate and went to his close stool. A few minutes later, his German valet heard 'a noise louder than the royal wind' and rushed into the room to find the King had fallen off the lavatory and on to the floor, hitting his head. He died of an aortic aneurysm.

William III's close stool. It is upholstered in crimson Genoa velvet and edged with a gold fringe and studs – this was a very luxurious if impractical toilet! (© Historic Royal Palaces)

HARRODS:
⚜ 'ALL THINGS FOR ALL PEOPLE, EVERYWHERE' ⚜

Harrod's motto is *Omnia Omnibus Ubique*, which is Latin for 'All Things for All People, Everywhere'. The world-famous store does seem to live up to its motto, as it attracts in the region of 15 million customers annually, and is London's largest retail space, spreading over seven floors. It is certainly worth a visit, even if it is just to admire the stunning architecture and interior design.

Charles Henry Harrod founded the store in 1834 and it probably never crossed his mind that it would become a British institution. The store moved to its current location in Knightsbridge after capitalising on brisk trade at a stall set up for the Great Exhibition of 1851. In 1898, one of the world's first escalators was installed; it was little more than a leather conveyor belt without steps, and brandy was offered to customers to revive them after their 'ordeal' when they reached the top!

The shop is famous for selling everything, including a baby elephant called Gertie, who was bought as a present for the then governor of California, Ronald Reagan. The elephant subsequently went to Sacramento Zoo. Harrods also sold an alligator, which was bought as a present for Noel Coward. Fortunately, selling live animals stopped in the 1970s. While in the toy department, author A.A. Milne found the teddy bear that his son, Christopher Robin Milne, named Winnie the Pooh.

Harrods. (© britainonview)

Harrods sells many luxury items, including a yacht with a price tag of £102 million, Ambootia Snowmist tea at £4,900 per kilogram, and a hand-made bed for £52,000. By comparison, the scale model, petrol-driven, black Mercedes SEL in the Toy Kingdom is a mere £6,995. There is even a pedestrian tunnel, which leads straight from the platform at Kensington Tube Station to the entrance of the store.

Lesser-known services include removals, for which they coined the motto, 'People vote out governments but Harrods moves in Prime Ministers', as well as valet parking and coat fittings for dogs. Until 1916, Harrods also sold pure cocaine to the public; customers were able to purchase kits with all the necessary accoutrements from the pharmacy to send to loved ones fighting on the front line, or for personal use at home if one felt the need. Evidently, entertainment then involved more than just a sing-song around the piano.

During the Second World War, the store thought it wise to set aside its wealthy, glamorous image and stopped selling luxury goods. Instead, it concentrated on producing uniforms, parachutes and parts for RAF Lancaster bombers, and gave up sections of the building to the Royal Canadian Air Force.

The store made the headlines in 2010, when long-term owner Mohammed Al Fayad sold the store to the Qatari Royal Family for £1.5 billion, then, in 2011, Harrods achieved a world record as the only stand-alone department store in the world to hit £1 billion in sales in a year. Harrods still maintains its high standards with rules for customers that must be strictly adhered to; shoppers must wear presentable clothes, photography is prohibited in certain departments, and unaccompanied children under the age of sixteen are not allowed in the store.

There is a life-sized statue of Dodi Fayed and Princess Diana at Door 3, and a memorial by the Egyptian escalators.

It takes around 12,000 light bulbs to illuminate the famous façade of the store every night.

❧ HATS OFF STRANGERS! ❧

The iconic building of the Houses of Parliament, otherwise known as the Palace of Westminster, stands as a symbol of Great Britain, and the decisions made in its corridors have shaped the country's past and present. This historic building is the meeting place of the House of Commons and the House of Lords. Much of how Parliament does its business has become established through continued use over the centuries. This is known as 'custom and practice'.

There are ancient rules and traditions that still have to be adhered to today in this glorious building, some of which seem to have no relevance to modern life and some that do: smoking has not been allowed in the chamber of the House of

Inside the House of Commons. (Library of Congress, LC-USZ62-97721)

Commons since the seventeenth century – members were permitted to take snuff instead and the doorkeepers still keep a 'snuff box' for this purpose; members may not eat or drink in the chamber though there is an exception to this rule, as the Chancellor of the Exchequer is allowed have an alcoholic drink while delivering the Budget statement; when the House of Commons is in session it is illegal for an MP to wear a full suit of armour; hats must not be worn, although they used to be worn when a point of order was being raised; members may not wear military decorations; members must not keep their hands in their pockets when in the Chamber (Andrew Robathan was heckled by opposing MPs when he did so on 19 December 1994); and animals are not allowed to enter the Palace of Westminster, with the exception of guide dogs for the blind, sniffer dogs, police horses and horses from the Royal stables.

It is not surprising that this largely male institution became the target of suffragette Emily Davidson when she hid in the Crypt under Westminster Hall for forty-eight hours, so that she could write 'House of Commons' as her address in the census of that year.

The most important part of the old palace was Westminster Hall. It is the oldest building in parliament and the only part of the ancient Palace of Westminster to survive in its almost original form.

When a new Speaker of the House of Commons is elected, other members physically drag the successful candidate to the Chair. This custom has its roots in the Speaker's function to communicate the Commons' opinions to the monarch.

The Houses of Parliament. (© VisitBritain / britainonview)

Historically, if the monarch did not agree with the message being communicated then the early death of the Speaker could follow – seven speakers were executed by beheading between 1394 and 1535. It is perhaps little wonder that speakers of old required some persuasion to accept the post. Before every sitting of the House, the Speaker's procession leaves the Speaker's House inside the Palace of Westminster and heads for the Commons chamber. Preceding the Speaker is the Serjeant at Arms carrying the Mace and other staff, including a doorkeeper, a chaplain, secretary and a trainbearer, follow behind. As the procession reaches the central lobby, a police officer on duty shouts, 'Hats Off Strangers!' which is the call for helmeted police officers and members of the public to remove their headgear as the procession passes.

Merchandise was sold in Westminster Hall in the 1290s and shops operated from around 1339. The Keeper of the Palace was entitled to the rent of 8*d* a year from each merchant renting a booth and to 4*d* a year from each merchant carrying his goods. By the reign of Richard II (1377-99), the Hall had become one of the chief centres of London life. Due to the presence of the law courts, the Hall also became a covered market for legal paraphernalia. Various shops and stalls jostled each other along the walls selling wigs, pens and other stationery. In the sixteenth century, the scholars of Westminster School were permitted to erect stalls to sell their books; by the late seventeenth century, drapers and ribbon counters were trading next to them. In 1666, there were forty-eight shops, some of which were combined to form larger premises. The stalls were removed for coronation banquets and restored afterwards.

From 1189 to 1821, Westminster Hall was the traditional venue for coronation banquets honouring newly crowned monarchs. The earliest recorded banquets were for Prince Henry (crowned whilst his father, Henry II, was still alive) in 1170 and of Richard the Lionheart in 1189.

The coronation feast of James II, held on 23 April 1685, was a huge event with an extensive menu of both hot and cold food. There was room for spectators in the galleries above the tables and prior to the feast, the law courts and shops were removed, and the Hall was furnished with the royal table at the top of the great stairs and two rows of tables stretching almost to the north door. Cutlery and dishes were stored in sixteen cupboards along the sides of the Hall.

On the day, participants were expected to arrive by 8 a.m. and were marshalled into the Hall in columns. When the King and Queen entered at 11.30 a.m., they were presented with the Sword of State and the coronation regalia, and were subsequently borne in procession to Westminster Abbey. Once the procession had departed, the tables were laid and cold food was set out. Once the coronation service in the Abbey was over, the King and Queen returned to the Hall for the banquet.

During the feast, the King and Queen sat at the royal table, wearing their crowns. At the other tables sat peers and peeresses, bishops, judges, barons, the King's Council, the Lord Mayor and the heralds; they were attended by about 200 servants, each nobleman also had one of his own servants present. The first course, which consisted of dishes of hot meat, was brought in by a procession of seventy-three people, including three officers on horseback.

❧ HAUNTED HAM HOUSE ❧

Ham House in Richmond-upon-Thames is allegedly one of Britain's most haunted houses. It is bursting with tales of those who died, but whose spirits have never left. Employees have said things happen in Ham House that cannot easily be explained, whether it is the appearance of mysterious footprints, the opening and closing of doors, ghostly sightings or objects that have inexplicably moved.

The extensive outbuildings include an orangery, icehouse, still house and dairy with cast-iron 'cows legs' supporting marble slabs. One lingering phantom at this seventeenth-century house is Elizabeth, Duchess of Lauderdale, who reputedly dabbled in witchcraft when she was alive. Footprints are sometimes heard in her bedchamber.

The earliest written account of a haunting is from Augustus Hare (1834–1903), who paid a visit to Ham House in 1879 and in *The Story of my Life* (1900) wrote:

'The Haunted Lane', *c.* 1889. (Library of Congress, LC-USZ62-49314)

There is a ghost at Ham. The old butler there had a little girl, she was then six years old. In the small hours of the morning, the child, waking up, saw an old woman scratching with her finger against the wall close to the fireplace. The girl was not at all frightened at first but sat up to look at her. The noise she made in doing this caused the old woman to look round and she came to the foot of the bed. She stared at the child long and fixedly. So horrible was her stare that the child was terrified and screamed and hid her face. People ran in and the child told what she had seen. The wall was examined where she had seen the figure scratching, and concealed in it were papers which proved that in that room, Elizabeth had murdered her first husband to marry the Duke of Lauderdale.

One young man living in the house had his heart broken by a maidservant who jilted him. He threw himself from a window to his death and it is said that if you listen carefully you may hear ghostly weeping on the terrace where his body was found …

Sometimes visitors have reported hearing a scratching noise coming from an upstairs room, which grows louder and closer. It approaches the stairs, comes down and suddenly stops. Witnesses have said it is the ghost of a King Charles spaniel. A member of staff reported that a visitor complained one afternoon that someone was letting a spaniel run around in the upper rooms. About five years ago, the skeleton of a dog was unearthed in the kitchen garden.

⁂ HER LONGING FOR GLOVES LED TO A COURT CASE ⁂

A report from the annals of the Old Bailey on 22 February 1716 stated:

> Elizabeth Wild; of the Parish of St Clement Danes, was indicted for privately stealing 3 pair of Silk Gloves, value 13s 6d out of the Shop of Charles Best, on the 6th of Jan last. The Prisoner came into the Shop for a pair of Black Silk Gloves, but not liking the first (according to the Custom of such Persons) others were shown her; in which time she had put up the Goods in the indictment, and then was very difficult, and nothing could please, and thereupon went away. But being call'd back, the Goods were found upon her; and the Prisoner begg'd for Mercy. In her Defence she said she long'd for them, and that she knew not why else she did it, not having any occasion as she knew of for them.

The jury found her guilty and fined her 10d.

At that time, 'privately stealing' five shillings or more worth of goods from a shop was designated as a capital offence.

❧ INN-TRIGUING LONDON ❧

'When you have lost your inns, drown your empty selves, for you will have lost the last of England.'

Joseph Hilaire Pierre René Belloc

Inn signs depict everything in history, from battles and heroes, to smuggling and sport, to royalty and explorers. The Romans built the first tavern, but the British were drinking a beer-like liquid as far back as the Bronze Age. These taverns were identified by hanging a garland of vine leaves outside on a pole, or, if there were facilities for playing chess, a chequer board was painted on the door post, hence the oldest inn sign, 'The Chequers'. In those days, an 'alehouse' could only serve ale, while a 'tavern' was the urban equivalent of a country inn, providing rooms for travellers as well as serving food and drink. Through time, the difference between these establishments has become indistinct; inns and taverns have evolved into hotels; alehouses into the modern pub. By the twelfth century, giving names to drinking establishments was commonplace.

So that the official 'Ale Taster' could identify them, King Richard II decreed in 1393 that, 'Whosoever shall brew ale in the town [London] with the intention of selling it must hang out a sign; otherwise he shall forfeit his ale'. Many signs have royal connections and the 'White Lion' dates from Edward IV's time, while the 'White Boar' was the emblem of Richard III. Before Henry VIII's reign, religious names like 'The Crossed Keys' – the emblem of St Peter – were popular. When Henry split with the Catholic Church, these were replaced with the more majestic 'Duke of Wellington', 'The Rose and Crown' and 'King's Head'.

An establishment in Fenchurch Street named the King's Head occupied the site later occupied by the London Tavern. The story goes that when Princess Elizabeth (who became Queen Elizabeth I), was released from the Tower in 1554, after being suspected of involvement in a plot against Queen Mary I, she went to a neighbouring church to offer thanks for her freedom. After that, she 'then proceeded to the King's Head to enjoy a somewhat plebeian dinner of boiled pork and pease-pudding.'

The most common pub name in the UK is 'The Red Lion' – there were around 630 at the last count. The name goes back to the days of James VI of Scotland. When he arrived in London to take the throne as James I of England, the new king ordered that the heraldic red lion of Scotland be displayed on all of the important buildings, including inns. The Red Lion is the nearest pub to the Houses of Parliament and Downing Street. Its division bell means that visiting MPs will not miss any important votes, and politically themed prints adorn the walls. The second longest-held beer license in London belongs to another Red Lion pub. This one has a black timber frontage and nestles in quaint, gas-lit Crown Passage near to St James's Palace. On the last Saturday in January, cavaliers in full costume visit the premises to bewail the death of their hero, King Charles I, who was executed on the balcony of the Banqueting House in Whitehall on 30 January 1649.

The King's Head in Acton. (© Mike Pickup)

'Old Dr Butler's Head' was named after Dr Butler, who was a fraudulent nerve specialist that believed in the efficacy of somewhat drastic 'cures'. They included dropping plague patients through a trapdoor into the River Thames from London Bridge, and treating epilepsy by firing a round of pistol shots near his unsuspecting patient in order to frighten the illness away. He also created the dubious 'Dr Butler's Purging Ale' – a potent drink with a powerful laxative effect. However, he still managed to impress King James I, who appointed him Court Physician. As time passed, the good doctor acquired several taverns, and made and sold 'medicinal ale', available only from those inns which displayed his head on their signs. The only one that survives today is in Mason's Avenue, on the site of the original, which was rebuilt after it was destroyed by the Great Fire in 1666.

'The Dove' in Hammersmith, once a coffee house, is an appealing riverside pub which has had several famous visitors including Graham Greene, Ernest Hemingway and Scottish poet James Thomson, writer of *Rule Britannia*, who lodged and died there. It is rumoured that Charles II and Nell Gwynne would use it as a venue for secret meetings. If they did, they would have revelled in what must be the cosiest bar in London. Measuring 4ft by 7ft 10in, it merits an entry in the *Guinness Book of Records* for the smallest bar in Britain.

The last galleried coaching inn in London is 'The George', which is tucked away in a cobbled courtyard off Borough High Street. It was rebuilt in 1676, after a fire swept through Southwark. It was one of many such inns in the area. In 1388, Chaucer began writing *The Canterbury Tales* in 'The Tabard'. It too was rebuilt after the fire of 1676, only to be demolished in the nineteenth century, despite a chorus of disapproval. Coaching inns declined with the advance of the railways, but The George was fortunate enough to avoid total destruction. The Great Northern Railway used it as a depot, demolishing part of it to build a warehouse. The Old Bar was the waiting room for coachmen and passengers, while the Middle Bar was the Coffee Room, a haunt of Charles Dickens. Another of Dickens' favoured drinking holes is 'The Grapes' in Narrow Street, in London's East End. Dickens immortalised it in *Our Mutual Friend*, referring to it as 'The Six Jolly Fellowship Porters pub'. He described it as, 'a tavern of dropsical appearance ... settled down into a state of hale infirmity. In its whole constitution it had not a straight floor and hardly a straight line; but it had outlasted – and clearly would yet outlast – many a better trimmed building.' Built in 1720, it outlasted many buildings in the area and survived the Industrial Revolution and the Blitz; it still stands to this day.

Chiswick's Strand on the Green is the location of the charming 'Bull's Head', complete with low ceilings, creaking floorboards, worn flagstones and a wonderful view of the Thames. This higgledy-piggledy pub has an appealing collection of different-sized rooms on various levels. Oliver Cromwell made the inn his headquarters during the Civil War and just across the river is Oliver's Island, where he allegedly took refuge. Yet another pub oozing history is 'The Shakespeare's Head' in Covent Garden, which is famed as being the birthplace of the sandwich. In the 1700s,

Ye Olde Cheshire Cheese inn sign. (© Mike Pickup)

Earl Sandwich was a keen gambler who, when snacking at gaming tables put meat between slices of bread to keep his fingers and the cards free from grease. 'The Shakespeare's Head' was home to an exclusive gaming society, the Beef Steak Club.

'The Mayflower' in Rotherhithe is the only pub in Britain licensed to sell both British and American postage stamps. It was from just outside the pub, at that time called 'The Shippe', that the *The Mayflower* was moored and left London in 1620 on its sixty-six-day journey to the New World. Its passengers were the first permanent European settlers in America. The pub took the name of the ship following a restoration in 1957, thanks to its associations with the historic voyage.

Ye Olde Cheshire Cheese sign.
(© Mike Pickup)

Ye Olde Cheshire Cheese, a Fleet Street pub rebuilt shortly after the Great Fire of 1666, lacks natural lighting, which gives it a certain gloomy charm. The vaulted cellars are thought to belong to a thirteenth-century Carmelite Monastery that once occupied the site. Regulars included such literary figures as Sir Arthur Conan Doyle, G.K. Chesterton and Charles Dickens. It is thought the pub is alluded to in *A Tale of Two Cities* when, following Charles Darnay's acquittal on charges of high treason, Sydney Carton invites him to dine with him. He leads him to Fleet Street 'up a covered way, into a tavern … where Charles Darnay was soon recruiting his strength with a good plain dinner and good wine'.

A broadside ballad from 1680 called 'A New Ballad of the Midwives Ghost', tells the story of how a midwife haunted the house where she died, until she was able to induce the new residents to dig up the bones of bastard children that she had murdered and buried. The final lines of the ballad insist upon the veracity of the tale and even that the children's bones may be seen for proof displayed at the Cheshire Cheese.

⁂ INSPIRING ORATORS AT SPEAKERS' CORNER ⁂

Inspiring orators can have their say at Hyde Park's Speakers' Corner every Sunday. Since 1872, after a riot about laws against buying and selling on a Sunday, it has been permissible for the public to exercise freedom of speech.

Hyde Park Corner around 1890–1900. (Library of Congress, LC-DIG-ppmsca-08575)

Not that this was well met by all in the beginning. *The Times*, reflecting the unease of the establishment of the day, declared after one such demonstration that, 'it is against all reason and all justice that motley crowds from all parts of the metropolis should take possession of Hyde Park, and interfere with the enjoyments of those to whom the Park more particularly belongs.'

However, writing about the same event, the *Reynolds' Weekly* newspaper of 29 July 1866 declared that despite the attempts of the police and troops to prevent them, 'the people have triumphed, in so far as they have vindicated their right to meet, speak, resolve, and exhort in Hyde Park.'

Some famous speakers include Karl Marx, Christabel Pankhurst and Baron Soper, a social activist who spoke so often that he was given the nickname 'Dr Soapbox'.

Hyde Park is one of London's finest landscapes. Around the time of the Domesday Book, about 900 years ago, the area belonged to monks from Westminster Abbey. Henry VIII acquired the park from the monks in 1536, because he was partial to deer hunting there. It was then a rural landscape of meadows dotted with trees and speckled with wild flowers. Boar and wild bulls roamed free. The Westbourne Stream, which now flows underground, crossed the area on its way between Hampstead and the Thames.

The Park remained a private hunting ground until James I came to the throne and permitted limited access. After that, when Charles I became king, he changed the nature of the park and opened it to the public. He also made a circular track called the 'Ring', where members of the royal court could drive their carriages.

In 1665, when the Great Plague wreaked havoc, many Londoners left the City to set up camp in Hyde Park. They believed it was far enough away from the City to avoid catching the disease.

When William and Mary came to the throne, they purchased Nottingham House on the western edge of the park for £20,000 in 1689, and renamed it Kensington Palace. They decided it would be their main London home. In order to travel from Kensington to Westminster, they created a processional route through Hyde Park. It had 300 oil lamps and was the first English road to be lit at night. It was called the 'Route de Roi', or King's Road, but the name became corrupted to Rotten Row. This bridle path through the park is popular today with riders, roller-bladers and joggers.

In 1728, Queen Caroline, wife of George II, decided to create Kensington Gardens from part of Hyde Park by separating the two parks with a ha-ha (a long ditch). She was also responsible for the creation of the Serpentine, an artificial lake. Caroline fancied herself a gardener and had some imaginative ideas. At that time, artificial lakes were usually long and straight and the Serpentine was one of the first lakes in England designed to look natural. It was soon copied in parks and gardens all over the country, and was the centrepiece of celebrations in 1814 for the British victory at the sea battle of Trafalgar.

Kensington Palace. (© Historic Royal Palaces)

Memorial in Hyde Park for the 7 July 2005 bombings. (geograph.org.uk © David Hawgood, Wikimedia Commons)

These days the Serpentine attracts a large number of wildfowl into the park. The lake also has beetles, bees and ground foraging insects, a vital component of the park ecosystem. The creation and protection of their habitats is important for the overall health of the park. Recent sightings have included a black swan, a buzzard and Egyptian geese.

When King George VI died in 1952, the code 'Hyde Park Corner' was used to inform the Government of his death.

In Hyde Park there is also a memorial to honour the victims of the London bombings of 7 July 2005, which was unveiled by the Prince of Wales and the Duchess of Cornwall in a ceremony which was also attended by the families of the fifty-two people killed. Located in the south-east corner of the park, the memorial comprises fifty-two stainless steel pillars collectively representing each of the victims, grouped together in four interlinking clusters reflecting the four locations of the disaster: on a tube train travelling between Liverpool Street and Aldgate; on one that had just left Edgware Road; on another between King's Cross and Russell Square; and the fourth on the top deck of a bus in Tavistock Square. Visitors can walk around and through the memorial, reading inscriptions marking the date, time and sites of the bombings on each pillar. There is a stainless steel plaque listing the names of the victims at the far eastern end of the memorial.

⚜ JELLIED EELS, WHITEBAIT, AND PIE AND MASH ⚜

Jellied eels were popular with Londoners because they were cheap and plentiful and in the early nineteenth century, eels were all that could survive in the polluted River Thames. Eels are still sold from street stalls today.

Whitebait was considered a more upmarket fare and ministerial whitebait dinners became popular in Greenwich during the Victorian times. The popularity started when a group of ministers sought to 'dine in a place of rest and of good repute'. Greenwich was chosen because of its convenience for London and it was decided that they should dine on whitebait at the newly opened Trafalgar Tavern. The shoals of tiny fish were caught locally in the Thames and within an hour after they had been caught, they were deep fried in lard until crisp, then dressed with lemon juice and cayenne pepper, served with brown bread and washed down with iced champagne.

Word of the Trafalgar Tavern spread, and more and more politicians visited. Until 1883, the whitebait dinner was an established annual tradition and barges brought ministers from Westminster. Charles Dickens based his wedding breakfast scene from *Our Mutual Friend* on the Hawke Room of the Trafalgar.

It is hard to believe now that for centuries oysters were part of the diet of London's poor. Sam Weller in *The Pickwick Papers* said, 'Poverty and oysters always seem to go together.'

Pie and mash, meanwhile, became a popular Cockney dish in the eighteenth century. Pies were the food *du jour* amongst the working classes as they were cheap, filling and could be eaten 'on the hoof'. The pies were originally made with eels, liquor made from eel gravy and flavoured with parsley sauce, but over time they were often made using minced beef and onion.

Men would walk around selling the pies, which were kept hot by means of a charcoal fire beneath the 'pie can', and there was a partition in the body of the can to separate hot and cold pies. Some of the sellers could earn around 1s 6d a day, while others earned no more than 4d. Summer fairs and races were the best places for them, and events like the Lord Mayor's show and the opening of parliament ensured their sales.

The sellers usually made the pies themselves. The meat was bought in 'pieces' at about 3d for a pound and about five dozen pies could be made at a time.

A typical recipe would be, 'a quartern of flour at 5d or 6d; 2lbs of suet at 6d; 1½lb meat at 3d, amounting in all to about 2s.' In addition, pepper, salt and eggs used to season and glaze them before cooking would cost about 2d. It was not a very profitable business. The usual quantity of meat in each pie was about half an ounce, while the gravy served with the pies consisted of 'salt and water browned'. A hole was made in the top of the pie and the gravy was poured in until the crust rose. Sometimes older meat could be sold, as the gravy disguised the flavour.

One seller moaned, 'The pies in Tottenham Court Road are highly seasoned. I bought one there the other day and it nearly took the skin off my mouth, it was full of pepper.' However, this could have been a case of sour grapes.

"COCKNEY'S"

TRADITIONAL
PIE
&
MASH

A pie and mash sign. (© VisitLondon / britainonview / Ingrid Rasmussen)

As the food increased in popularity, shops began to spring up to cater to demand. The longest running is Goddards, which opened in Deptford in 1890 and still operates in Greenwich today making old-fashioned, hand-made pies.

❧ JONGY THE LEMUR AND ELTHAM PALACE ❧

First recorded in 1086 in the Domesday Book, Eltham Manor was owned by the Bishop of Bayeux, William the Conqueror's brother. In 1305, the house was presented to Edward II, who subsequently passed it on to his queen, Isabella, and for more than two centuries it was a favoured royal residence. Today, little remains of the original palace apart from the moated enclosure, the bridge, the foundations of the adjoining royal apartments and the Great Hall, which was built in the 1470s by Edward IV. During the Civil War, soldiers were posted there to stop trouble in the area. However, the soldiers were on the side of Parliament, not the King, and a royal palace was 'fair game', so they ransacked it.

The Great Hall, with a dais at one end and a beautiful wooden, hammer-beam roof, was the dining room for the royals and a place for entertainment. During Christmas of 1482, according to records, 2,000 people enjoyed a great feast here.

Eltham Palace. (www.visitgreenwich.co.uk)

As time passed, this glamorous hall was used as a barn, but was later restored to its former glory by the Ancient Monuments Division and the Courtauld family.

During King Henry VIII's reign, an intricate network of tunnels was created to take waste away from the kitchens while other tunnels, which were flushed with clean water, served the toilets or 'garderobes'.

The next big change to the palace came centuries later in the 1930s, when the wealthy and glamorous couple, Stephen and Virginia Courtauld, took on a long lease of Eltham Palace. Their fortune came from manufacture and production of man-made fibres including 'Courtelle', an acrylic yarn resembling wool. With their wealth, generated by shares Stephen had inherited, he devoted his time to pursuing a variety of cultural interests and was financial director of Ealing Film Studios. They built a new Art Deco style house next to the remains of Eltham Palace. Some people thought the design of their new home was marvellous, but to others it resembled a 'cigar factory'.

Their house included new gadgets of the day, including electric fires and a loudspeaker system that could broadcast music throughout the whole of the ground floor. Many rooms reflected the 'Cunard style' made fashionable by cruise liners featuring built-in furniture. Guest bedrooms were styled to be like cabins and equipped with electric heaters, writing desks and wardrobes with sliding doors. There was an internal telephone system and payphone, so that guests could make external calls at their own expense. Although this seems overly frugal, at the time phone calls were extremely expensive. Socket fittings in every room allowed for a cleaning hose to be connected to suck dirt down to a central vacuum cleaner located in the basement. The luxury continued with a gold-plated, en-suite bathroom featuring an onyx bath.

The entrance hall contained a circular, hand-knotted replica original carpet, which is now on show in the Victoria and Albert Museum, while the boudoir has a leather patchwork map showing the local Eltham area as it was in the 1930s, with Eltham Palace in the centre. A hidden door in this room links to the library. On the terrace there are reliefs illustrating the couple's interest in mountaineering, badminton, quoits, gardening and yachting.

Stephen and Virginia enjoyed hosting parties at their home and their guests would be introduced to their ring-tailed lemur called Jongy. The pet lemur had his own heated quarters and a bamboo ladder that allowed him to climb down to the ground floor where he was fed. Jongy was purchased at Harrods in 1923 and lived with the Courtaulds for fifteen years, accompanying the couple on their travels.

When Stephen Courtauld sponsored the 1930–31 British Arctic Air Route Expedition, the Courtaulds held a farewell lunch on board their yacht on the morning of departure, where Jongy bit Percy Lemon's hand (the expedition's wireless operator) and severed an artery. He was treated with iodine, but Lemon proved allergic to the antiseptic. It took him three months to recover and delayed the expedition. Jongy died at Eltham Palace in 1938.

The Courtaulds left Eltham in 1944 and the site was then occupied by army educational units until 1992. English Heritage assumed management of the palace in 1995. Today, the gardens are a rare and fine example of the 1930s design. The fact that they incorporate elements of the medieval palace adds a further intriguing dimension.

KEW GARDENS:
❧ COFFEE BUSHES, PHEASANTS AND LEMON GRASS ❧

In the early 1750s, forward-thinking Princess Augusta, mother of King George III, started the creation of an ambitious 9-acre garden around the palace at Kew. By 1754, 110 acres were enclosed by hedges, the lake and mound finished, and the Chinese and bell temples had been built. William Chambers was employed as architect – planning and overseeing the construction of buildings such as the orangery and the pagoda. By 1768, the herbaceous collection contained over 2,700 species.

The gardens are now a major international attraction and a World Heritage Site, comprising 132 hectares of glorious gardens. It is an inspirational place to visit and somewhere to revel in extravagant vistas. The arboretum stretches across two thirds of the gardens and contains over 14,000 specimens of more than 2,000 species, including trees dating back to the early eighteenth century. Kew's Treetop Walkway allows visitors to stroll through the tree canopy 18m above ground. A sweet chestnut tree is probably the oldest in the gardens, while the 'Old Lions' are some of the few remaining trees known to have been planted in Princess Augusta's original garden, around 1762. These include the maidenhair tree (*Gingko biloba*), the Japanese pagoda tree and the Oriental plane tree. The unluckiest tree in the collection must be a Corsican Pine, because early in the twentieth century, a light aircraft crashed into it and took out the top of the tree. Since then it has been struck by lightning on several occasions, the last of which was in 1992, and scars on the trunk serve as a reminder.

Kew has many iconic buildings, including a collection of glasshouses. The modern Princess of Wales Conservatory, opened by Diana, Princess of Wales in July 1987, and the Davies Alpine House are award-winning designs, which use latest technologies to control and regulate temperatures. The controls enable staff to maintain ten different environments inside the glasshouses, ranging from dry desert heat to moist, tropical rainforest. The giant Amazonian water lily was a big attraction for the Victorians and is still popular today, while cacti, ferns and the Titan arum, characterised by its foul smell, can be seen here too.

In the eye-catching, Grade I listed, tropical Palm House around a quarter of the plants displayed are threatened in their natural environment, as are more than

Kew Museum. (© Mike Pickup)

half of the cycads, which are living fossils of the tropics. There are coffee bushes, jade vines, the Madagascar periwinkle and the coco de mer, which is the world's largest seed and looks rather like a human bottom, weighing up to 30kg. The seed is native to the Seychelles and comes from a fan palm that grows only on the tiny island of Praslin.

There are fourteen different gardens within Kew to explore, each one providing a different experience. The Rose Garden has masses of old-fashioned red and creamy roses climbing the pergolas, the Grass Garden has 550 species of grass, and the Woodland Garden delights the senses with a sheer abundance of primroses, daffodils and dog's tooth violets. One can view a spectacularly grand tapestry in the Secluded Garden, providing a sensory voyage of discovery.

The lush and verdant plant life is home to 128 species of our feathered friends, including woodpeckers, great crested grebes, herons and pheasants, which were introduced to the dells. Kew supports an extraordinarily diverse range of wildlife, found mostly in the conservation area surrounding Queen Charlotte's Cottage. The location is mostly woodland, and throughout spring the ground is carpeted in a marvellous display of bluebells, wild garlic and snowdrops. Dead trees are left where they fall as decaying crevices provide excellent feeding and nesting opportunities for birds and roosting places for Kew's many bats. More species depend on dying or dead wood than on living trees.

In 1876, Kew was given 70,000 rubber tree seeds from the Amazon. Only 2,800 germinated, but from them, seedlings sent to Malaysia flourished, starting the massive rubber industry. There are also African oil palms, from which the oil can be pressed from the flesh to make soap and candles, and oil from the stone's kernel can be used for edible oils and fats.

The Waterlily House is also a listed building and dates back to 1852. It is Kew's hottest and most humid environment, housing tropical, ornamental aquatic plants and climbers. There are Nymphaea waterlilies, a giant Victoria cruziana, sacred lotus, papyrus, gourds, loofah, as well as economically important plants including rice, bananas, taro, sugar cane and lemon grass.

In the sunken Nosegay Garden, plants are selected primarily for their medicinal qualities, reflecting the seventeenth-century use of fragrant flowers to help cover bad odours. Plants in nosegays included sage, artemisia and bergamot, all of which still grow here. Plant labels explain what the purpose of these herbs was. Common marigold is said to comfort 'hearts and spirits', while borage 'relieves sorrow.' Digitalis purpurea was used to treat heart problems, while rosemary has been used medicinally from ancient times to improve cognitive performance and mood. St John's wort was, and still is, used as an antidepressant, while the sign on the Lady's Mantle tells us, 'It helpeth also such maides or women that have over great flagging breasts, causing them to grow less and hard'.

KEW PALACE:
❧ QUEEN CHARLOTTE'S CHAIR AND WITCH MARKS ❧

Kew Palace served as a royal retreat for the prodigious family of King George III and Queen Charlotte. It also served for a time as a sanatorium for the 'Mad King'. During one of these bouts of so-called insanity (thought by medical experts today to have been caused by porphyria) the king insisted on ending every sentence with the word 'peacock'. He even tried to open parliament with a speech that began, 'My lords and peacocks …' He also started wearing a pillowcase on his head.

When Queen Charlotte became ill it was thought that a few days in the clean air of Kew would improve her health, but her daughter, Princess Elizabeth, was not particularly impressed with the palace, and complained that it was damp and unfit to house her mother during what was to be her final bout of illness. The Queen's condition deteriorated and she contracted pneumonia. In the last few days of her life, she found it difficult to lie down and was more comfortable sitting in what is now known as 'Queen Charlotte's Chair', where she eventually died at 1 p.m. on Tuesday, 17 November 1818, surrounded by four members of her family. The chair is on display today. Queen Charlotte's granddaughter, Queen Victoria, said that she 'wished the room to be kept as it had been during her grandmother's lifetime'. These words are on a plaque beside the fireplace.

There are 'witch marks' carved in the attics of Kew Palace to ward off evil spirits. When the palace was built, people were particularly superstitious and believed that evil influences or witches could enter the house disguised as cats or frogs and cast spells on people while they slept. The original carpenters who

Queen Charlotte's Cottage. (© Historic Royal Palaces)

Witch marks at Kew Palace. (© Gilly Pickup)

made the roof carved special, secret signs near windows, doors and fireplaces to ward off evil'.

The nearby Queen Charlotte's Cottage was used by the royals for taking tea during walks in the gardens and for housing royal pets. Queen Caroline had kept tigers at Richmond, but George III and Queen Charlotte contented themselves with rather more docile pets, including oriental cattle and colourful Tartarian pheasants, the descendants of which are still to be seen in this quiet area of the gardens. From the early 1790s, kangaroos (the first to arrive in England) were successfully bred in the Queen's Cottage paddock and by the early nineteenth century there were eighteen kangaroos.

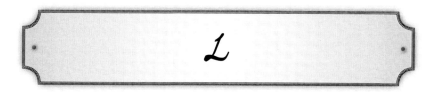

L

⚘ LOOK OUT BEHIND YOU! ⚘

Joseph Grimaldi, famous performer and clown, still takes the occasional spectral curtain call at the seventeenth-century Sadler's Wells Theatre. Grimaldi's last request was that his head be severed from his body before burial – which might account for his disembodied, white-painted face having been seen several times watching a show over the shoulders of the audience in one of the theatre's boxes. Grimaldi does not confine his eerie antics to just one of London's theatres; his head has also been seen floating around the Theatre Royal in Drury Lane, where he is said to prod unsuspecting actors and staff.

The Theatre Royal is said to be home to a veritable flock of phantoms, one of whom is Dan Leno, a former pantomime dame, who went mad before his

Theatre Royal, Drury Lane. (© Gilly Pickup)

death in 1904. His ghost is said to push actors or tug their wigs as they stand in the wings. On other occasions, a drumming sound can be heard coming from the dressing room where he used to rehearse his famous clog-dancing routine.

Another of the Theatre Royal's apparitions is the Man in Grey, complete with powdered wig, three-cornered hat, ruffled shirt and riding cape. He limps from one side of the upper circle to the other – then walks straight through the wall. Because he invariably appears in daylight, the Man in Grey has been witnessed by countless people. His identity is a mystery, but builders renovating the theatre in the 1870s knocked down the wall that the phantom walks through and found a skeleton, with a dagger protruding from his ribcage and shreds of grey cloth hanging from his bones. Despite his apparently bloody end, the Man in Grey is said to bring luck as he only appears at the beginning of a successful run, including *The King and I*, *South Pacific* and every cast change of the long-running *Miss Saigon*. He is even said to move actors into a better position on stage.

Her Majesty's Theatre was built in 1897 for actor-manager, Sir Beerbohm Tree, and he made several appearances on stage. He used to like to watch performances from the top box, 'stage right', and this is the centre for manifestations reported today. Occupants of the box have regularly complained of cold spots and have said that the door to the box suddenly opens of its own accord. The activities are not restricted to this area and in the 1970s, during a performance of *Cause Célèbre*, the cast of the play, which included the actress Glynis Johns, apparently saw the ghost walk across the theatre at the back of the stalls and disappear.

✻ MIND THE GAP! ✻

The phrase 'Mind the Gap!' originated on the Northern line in 1968, and was an automated warning for passengers about the space between the train and the platform edge.

London is home to the world's oldest underground railway. Central London Railway was originally called the Twopenny Tube because that was the cost of the fare, and it has since led to the whole London Underground system being nicknamed the 'Tube'. On average, 2.7 million Tube journeys are made every day, and Victoria is the busiest station with approximately 76.5 million passengers per year.

True to London Underground's tradition of innovation, a spiral escalator was installed in 1907 at Holloway Road Station, but despite such inventiveness, conventional linear escalators were favoured for the rest of the network. Only a

Park Royal Tube Station. (© Mike Pickup)

small section of the spiral escalator now remains – in the custody of the London Transport Museum at Acton Depot.

The first escalator with steps was installed at Earl's Court Station in 1911. It was such a novelty that people made special journeys just to try it. It is recorded that a man named 'Bumper Harris', who had an artificial leg, was employed to travel up and down the escalator all day in order to prove to the scared commuters that if he could use it without mishap, then anyone could. This, however, may be no more than a tall story. Seventy-nine-year-old Prime Minister Palmerston refused to travel on the first underground railway 'on the grounds that at his age it was advisable to stay above ground as long as possible'. Each of the 400 or so escalators travel the equivalent of two round-the-world trips in kilometres every week.

Before she became Queen, Princess Elizabeth travelled on the London Underground for the first time in May 1939, accompanied by her sister Princess Margaret and her governess, Marion Crawford, known as 'Crawfie'. They went to the YWCA canteen in Tottenham Court Road because their grandmother, Queen Mary, wanted them to experience the 'real London'.

However, this particular trip was not successful as Princess Elizabeth, unused to serving herself, left her pot of tea behind on the counter. The woman in charge shouted, 'If you want it, come and get it yourself.' They were soon recognised, as two immaculately dressed children accompanied by a governess and a detective stood out in a YWCA canteen. Crowds gathered and the detective had to call a car and whisk them away, so the experience was not repeated.

Not only did the Tube help 200,000 inner city children escape to the country in the Second World War, but underground stations sheltered thousands of civilians every night during the Blitz. On 27 September 1940, a census found that 177,500 Londoners were sleeping in Tube stations. With so many people seeking shelter, London Underground installed 22,000 bunk beds, washroom facilities and even ran trains that supplied 7 tons of food and 2,400 gallons of tea and cocoa every night. Before long, some stations offered libraries, evening classes, films and musical evenings.

There are reports of parts of the London Underground being haunted. Anne Naylor, who was murdered in 1758, is said to haunt Farringdon station, and there are reports of passengers hearing blood-curdling screams as the last train leaves. Covent Garden station has a male phantom, William Terris, who met an untimely death in 1897. He is well dressed and those who have seen him say he disappears very suddenly. Some staff members have even refused to work at the station because of him.

Hundreds of forgotten items are left behind on London's public transport every month, not just on the Tube, but in buses and taxis too. The most common objects people leave behind are keys, laptops, mobile phones, suitcases and umbrellas when it is raining. In 2010, more than 38,000 books, almost 29,000 bags

Second World War air-raid shelter. (Wikimedia Commons by the National Archives and Records Administration)

and 28,000 items of clothing were left behind by passengers. The more bizarre items include a Rolex watch and a bag containing £10,000 in cash. There was also a lawnmower and human skulls, the latter left behind by a professor who used them to demonstrate in lectures rather than more grisly motives. Breast implants were left behind by a courier on his way to a Harley Street clinic. It does make you wonder who left behind the stuffed fish, the outboard motor, harpoon gun, inflatable doll and Tibetan bell …

After three months, if inclaimed, items of value are given to the British Red Cross and Salvation Army. Data is wiped from phones and laptops, then they are auctioned off and the profits put back into running the operation.

❧ MRS SALMON'S WAXWORK SHOP ☙

London has offered every kind of entertainment imaginable to paying customers throughout its history. Oddities and curiosities of every kind were on commercial display, from hermaphrodites and dwarves to acrobatic monkeys and animals who could do arithmetic and tell fortunes. Hand-to-hand combat, puppet shows, conjurers, strange inventions and quack doctors were all popular amusements. If the real thing was not available, there were always waxworks offered as a substitute. Mrs Salmon's Fleet Street exhibition of historical tableaux and horrific scenes in wax lasted for more than a century.

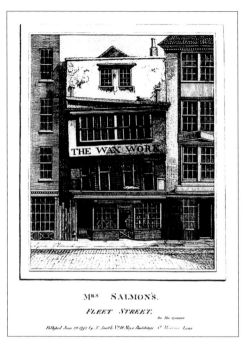

MRS SALMON'S.

FLEET STREET.

See The Spectator

Published June 28 1793 by J. Smith, No 18, Mays Buildings St Martins Lane

The shop can be found by walking up Inner Temple Lane to the gatehouse at its northern end, one of the few survivors of the Great Fire of London. For a while, part of the building was a tavern called the Hand Inn. Later, it was renamed the Prince's Arms, perhaps in honour of James I's short-lived son, Henry, Prince of Wales (1594–1612). The elegantly panelled main room on the first floor had a fine Jacobean plaster ceiling with the

Fleet Street Waxworks copper plate etching – this example being bound into Antiquities of London and its Environs, around 1800. (Wikimedia Commons)

Prince of Wales' feathers in the centre and the letters 'PH', for Prince Henry. It was thought that the house was originally built for the Council of the Duchy of Cornwall and that Prince Henry used the room on the first floor after he became Prince of Wales in 1610.

From 1795, the premises, now called 'The Fountain', were leased by Mrs Salmon to house her collection of waxworks, where it remained for several years. People queued to see exhibits, which included a waxwork of Mother Shipton driven by clockwork that kicked people as they left the shop, thanks to hidden treadles under the floorboards. Another waxwork depicted Charles I's execution and there was one of Hermione, a Roman Lady, whose father offended the Emperor. He was sentenced to death by starvation but was preserved by sucking his daughter's breast. Also included in her collection was a series of 'anatomical' waxes alongside tableaux, including one of 'Shepherds and Shepherdesses making violent love'.

A young Charles Dickens was a frequent visitor to Mrs Salmon's waxworks shop and he even sent his fictional David Copperfield 'to see some perspiring waxworks in Fleet Street'. After Mrs Salmon died, the exhibition was sold and removed to Water Lane.

⚜ MURDER: THE ARISTOCRAT AND THE BUTLER ⚜

Lord William Russell was murdered while sleeping in his house in Norfolk Street, Park Lane in 1840. The following morning his housemaid, Sarah Mancer, woke to discover the lower floors of the house in complete disarray with items spread over the floors, cupboard doors open and drawers which had been emptied. She thought that a robbery must have taken place, so she ran to alert the valet. François Benjamin Courvoisier was already awake and dressed, and after seeing the state of the house agreed that there must have been a break-in. Together they ran to their employer's bedroom. Courvoisier opened the door and made to open the shutters as he always did, while Sarah Mancer noticed immediately that Russell was dead. His throat was cut and he was soaked in blood.

When the police arrived, Courvoisier drew their attention to marks on the pantry door which he said must have been where the robbers entered. However, the police had other ideas and concluded that the 'robbery' was a set-up to take suspicion away from a member of the household. Some gold and silver items and a £10 banknote were missing; though later some of the articles were discovered elsewhere in the house. Other items were found hidden in Courvoisier's pantry, which turned suspicion onto him. More evidence developed with the discovery of a screwdriver in his possession that matched the marks on the pantry door, as well as marks left by the forcing of the silverware drawer.

After the discovery, Prime Minister Melbourne informed the Queen that his Lordship was found 'quite cold and stiff' and the wounds 'had nearly divided his head from his body.'

Courvoisier was sent to trial, but there was doubt over whether his guilt could be proved. His counsel, Charles Phillips, hinted that the maid may be the guilty party until an inventory indicated that further items of silverware were missing. Silver matching the description was located in a French hotel in Leicester Square. When his barrister told Courvoisier of this, he confessed to theft and the murder, but maintained his plea of 'not guilty' in court. The legal interest in the case arises from Phillips approaching the judge for guidance. He was forcefully told he could not ask for such advice, so he continued the defence, knowing that his client was guilty.

The Times reported the incident:

> The case brought to trial was weak, based heavily on flimsy and circumstantial evidence, and public sympathy seemed to go towards the handsome 23-year Courvoisier and an acquittal seemed likely. Dramatically, an eleventh hour witness came forward; a Frenchwoman from a dingy Leicester Square hotel where Courvoisier had once waited tables. She testified that he left a parcel with her around the day of the murder. Inside police found several items stolen from Lord William's home, including much silver plate. The shaken defense counsel

can only lamely suggest the evidence might have been planted in such a disreputable hostelry. The finding turned the day against the accused. The Lord Chief Justice wept while pronouncing the death sentence while Courvoisier showed no emotion.

It emerged in Courvoisier's confession that Russell had discovered his silverware thefts and ordered Courvoisier to resign from the household. After his sentence was passed, Courvoisier said:

His lordship was very cross with me and told me I must quit his service. As I was coming upstairs from the kitchen I thought it was all up with me; my character was gone, and I thought it was the only way I could cover my faults by murdering him. This was the first moment of any idea of the sort entering my head. I went into the dining room and took a knife from the sideboard. I do not remember whether it was a carving knife or not. I then went upstairs, I opened his bedroom door and heard him snoring in his sleep; there was a rushlight in his room burning at this time. I went near the bed by the side of the window, and then I murdered him. He just moved his arm a little; he never spoke a word.

Before he was hanged outside Newgate Prison on 6 July 1840, the valet announced that his conscience had told him, 'Thou art doing wrong', but he continued; 'I hardened myself against this voice and threw myself on my victim.' A crowd said to exceed 40,000 people watched the execution, with Charles Dickens and William Makepeace Thackeray among the audience. After the event, the latter wrote an anti-capital punishment essay called 'On Going to See a Man Hanged'. He wrote: 'I came away that morning with a disgust for murder, but it was for the murder I saw done … I feel myself shamed and degraded at the brutal curiosity that took me to that spot.'

⚓ NELSON'S COLUMN

Horatio Nelson was not comme-
morated for his battles until almost
forty years after his death at Trafalgar,
when Nelson's Column was built.
Although members of Parliament
had voted through a few thousand
pounds, most of the money came
from individuals generously
donating money to the fund set up
for building it. Nicholas I (Czar of
Russia) made a donation that was
almost a quarter of the £47,000 bill,
which in today's money would be
around £3 million.

The sculptor, Edward Hodges
Baily, created the 18-ton statue in
three main sections, consisting of
the lower body, upper body and
left arm, which clasps a mighty 8ft
bronze sword. Even the word 'Nile',
engraved into the King's Medal,

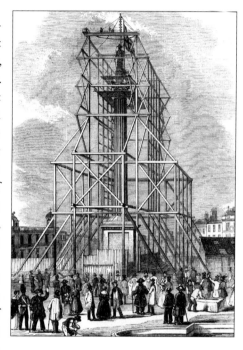

Nelson's Column under construction in Trafalgar
Square, c. 1840.

is still visible, serving as a reminder of the epic victory at the Battle of the
Nile, in 1798. When work was finished on the Corinthian column, fourteen
stonemasons who had worked on the structure had a dinner party on top,
complete with table and chairs, before Nelson was hoisted to stand on the
pinnacle. They obviously did not suffer from vertigo, because the monument is
169ft 3in (51.6m) tall measuring from the bottom of the pedestal to the top of
Nelson's hat.

The bronze lions at the foot of the column were the work of Sir Edwin
Landseer, and depict Admiral Nelson's victories at the battle of the Nile, Cape
St Vincent, Copenhagen and Trafalgar. They were created by using a dead lion
as a model. As he worked, the animal gradually decomposed and the smell was

so terrible that his neighbours called the police to investigate where it was coming from.

⚜ NEWGATE'S BLACK DOG ⚜

Amen Court (EC4) is not far from Paternoster Row, where monks would finish their Pater Noster, a Christian prayer, on Corpus Christi Day before walking to St Paul's Cathedral. When they reached the corner of the Row, they said 'Amen', which is how it got its name.

There is a high wall at the back of the Amen Court, behind which stood Newgate Prison and it shielded the narrow passageway of Deadman's Walk, so-called because that was the route taken by condemned prisoners on their way to execution. It is thought that this section of the wall is haunted by a manifestation known as the 'Black Dog of Newgate', which crawls along the wall, snarling, before disappearing. Its manifestations are always accompanied by a nauseous smell.

The Black Dog's origins are said to date back to the reign of Henry III, when a famine struck London and prisoners incarcerated in Newgate Prison, faced with the prospect of starvation, turned to cannibalism as a means of survival. The Black Dog is thought to be the ghost of a prisoner incarcerated for being a wizard, who was eaten by other prisoners. The spirit of this sorcerer returned in the form of a huge black dog, patrolling the prison and looking for revenge. It is said that some prisoners were torn limb from limb by the beast, while others died of fright when they heard its ghostly panting. Those who survived the first nights of its lust for vengeance became so terrified that they killed their guards and escaped.

When the prison was demolished in the early 1900s, no one expected the Black Dog to reappear. However, people walking in Amen Court at night have reported seeing a black shape, slithering across the top of the wall before disappearing.

NO HUMMING, SINGING
⚜ OR WHISTLING ALLOWED IN THIS STREET ⚜

Lord George Cavendish grew tired of passers-by throwing rubbish – particularly oyster shells – into his garden at Burlington House, Piccadilly. He decided to commission an architect, Samuel Ware, to design a covered promenade of shops over the garden area to stop it from happening. Rather than say he wanted the shops built to keep his garden tidy, he declared they were 'for the gratification of the public and to give employment to industrious females'. Burlington Arcade

Burlington Arcade. (© VisitLondon / britainonview / Ingrid Rasmussen)

is the result and is the longest covered shopping street in Britain. It opened on 20 March 1819, and is now a designated historic and architectural masterpiece.

Originally there were forty-seven leaseholders, six of whom were 'industrious females', but in accordance with the rules of the day, even the male milliners and corsetières were addressed as 'Madame'. Many of the tenants and their families lived in cramped conditions above and below their shops, sharing the space with their stock.

The tradition of uniformed beadles continues and they still patrol the arcade. Originally, they were recruited from Lord Cavendish's family regiment, the 10th Hussars. These liveried guards, wearing traditional Edwardian frock coats and gold braided top hats, are now synonymous with its heritage. The task of the Beadles, the smallest private police force in existence, is to discourage unruly behaviour and they have the authority to eject from the arcade anyone who runs, carries large packages, opens an umbrella, whistles, plays a musical instrument, hums or sings. No babies' prams are allowed inside either. In the early 1980s, a Beadle told someone off for whistling before realising it was Paul McCartney. It is not documented whether he was ejected or not.

There have been some changes in the lives of the Beadles since the early days. For instance, they no longer enjoy the luxury of resting in the armchairs originally positioned at either end of the arcade and designated for their use. Nor are they required to ring a hand bell to announce close of trading, as they did in the nineteenth and early twentieth centuries. In the 1880s, the curfew was 8 p.m.

During the Second World War, there was considerable architectural damage to the Piccadilly end of the arcade when it was stuck by bombs; restoration work was completed in the 1950s.

An admirer once bought Fred Astaire nine pairs of gold and striped slippers at the arcade. The designer later spotted Astaire checking the window displays and guessed what he was looking for. 'I stood in the doorway and as he approached, I cast my eyes down to where the slippers were displayed.' Astaire roared with laughter and bought several more pairs.

Film star Ann Todd telephoned Richard Ogden, an established jeweller in the arcade, to ask if he would consider closing his shop for a brief visit by Ingrid Bergman, who did not wish to attract any publicity. He immediately agreed and positioned one of his staff outside the door to deter any would-be customers. When an elderly woman approached, he explained, as instructed, that the shop was temporarily closed, but added, 'Have a look, can you see who is in there?' Peering through she said delightedly, 'Of course I can see, it is dear Mr Ogden.'

In June 1964, a spectacular robbery took place. A Jaguar Mark X drove down the arcade at high speed, the first and only four wheels ever to enter. Six masked men, armed with axe handles and iron bars, smashed the windows of the Goldsmiths and Silversmiths Association shop. They stole jewellery valued at £35,000 before making their escape by reversing back up the arcade. The robbers were never caught and bollards at the Burlington Gardens entrance were subsequently introduced.

During the Crimean War, Lord Panmure (Minister for War) requested designs from the jeweller, Hancocks, for a new award. Prototypes were submitted to Queen Victoria, and in March 1856 she approved the designs for the Victoria Cross. The first presentation took place on 26 June 1857, when the Queen decorated sixty-two soldiers and sailors. Since the inception of the award, Hancocks have produced every one of the 1,350 VCs issued.

The 150th anniversary celebration was only the third social function in the Burlington Arcade's history. The first was to mark the passing of the Parliamentary Reform Bill in 1832; the second, in 1954, to celebrate the rebuilding of the north end destroyed by war damage. On 21 May 1969, the guest of honour, Princess Alexandra, unveiled a commemorative plaque at an evening reception. The plaque was designed and moulded by the Joshua Wedgwood studios to mark the 150th milestone.

OLD OPERATING THEATRE,
⚕ MUSEUM AND HERB GARRET ⚕

St Thomas' Hospital in Southwark, located just south of London Bridge, was in existence well before 1215. This mixed order of Augustinian monks and nuns dedicated to Thomas Becket provided shelter and treatment for the poor, sick and homeless. In the fifteenth century, Richard Whittington endowed a laying-in ward for unmarried mothers and by the 1500s, it was described as a 'bawdy' house, possibly because it treated prostitutes and their clients for sexually transmitted diseases. Southwark was London's red-light district in those days.

This unique museum incorporating the only surviving nineteenth-century operating theatre is accessed via a spiral stairway and is located in the garret of St Thomas' Church, on the original site of St Thomas' Hospital. Rediscovered in 1956, the oak-beamed garret was used by the apothecary of St Thomas' Hospital to store and cure medicinal herbs.

The Apothecary's Act of 1815 meant apprentice apothecaries had to attend public hospitals, resulting in students coming to watch operations. This created a need for space and an environment where students could learn new techniques. Previously, operations had taken place on the ward in front of the other patients, but this became impractical in restricted ward space, so part of the herb garret roof was converted into a purpose-built operating theatre. Although not heated or ventilated, it provided an ideal – though small – area for demonstrating surgical skills. Spectators witnessed surgery from the observation stands.

Until 1846, operations were performed without anaesthesia or antiseptics. Surgeons depended on swift techniques and could perform an amputation in a minute or less, while alcohol or opiates were used to dull the patient's senses. Thereafter, ether or chloroform started to come into use. Patients endured the audience to their distress because they received medical treatment from some of London's best surgeons, which otherwise they could not afford. Wealthy patients would have been operated on at home, probably on the kitchen table, though this would have been their choice.

On 21st December 1846, Dr Robert Liston, known as the 'fastest knife in Britain', amputated butler Frederick Churchill's leg at University College Hospital in a record twenty-eight seconds, the first operation to be carried out in Britain under anaesthesia. Liston held the scalpel in his teeth while sewing. Liston's admirers claimed that 'the gleam of his knife was followed so instantaneously by the sounds of sawing as to make the two actions appear almost simultaneous'.

Risk of death at the hands of a surgeon was increased by the lack of understanding of the causes of infection. Contemporary accounts record surgeons wearing frock coats 'stiff and stinking with pus and blood'. Beneath the table was a sawdust box for collecting blood. The death rate was further heightened by the shock of the operation and because the procedures were a last resort, patients were severely weakened by the illness.

Today's visitors can browse the natural remedies, including snail water for venereal disease, 'bladderwrack' used as a remedy for goitre and tuberculosis, and a nerve-shredding array of amputation knives. In those days, surgical instruments were not sterilised, but reused from patient to patient, allowing infection to spread.

The operating theatre had closed down before antiseptic surgery came into being. The majority of cases were for amputations or superficial complaints because without sterile conditions, it was too dangerous to do internal operations.

Looking at patient notes, one can see how far medicine has progressed since the 1800s:

ELIZABETH RAIGEN - PATIENT'S NOTES
To Be Published in THE LANCET APRIL - MAY 1824
Elizabeth Raigen, age 60, was admitted 19th April 1824, with a compound fracture of tibia and fibula and an extensive Wound of the integuments (skin). The accident happened in consequence of a heavy carriage passing obliquely over the leg. On examination it was found she had received an oblique fracture of the tibia and fibula, just above the ankle, and therefore not including the joint in the accident. The wound it was supposed was made by the grazing of the wheel, which extended from about three inches below the head of the tibia to just below the ankle joint, ending opposite the tarsal bones, (the wound was very clearly cut) no large artery had been wounded; but they stated she had lost a considerable quantity of blood immediately after the accident …

By order of Mr. Green the edges of the wound were brought together as well as they could by adhesive straps, and the leg was laid on a pillow. She did not sleep during the night, and was very restless. At 12 o' clock reaction began, and the leg became hot. At this time her pulse was about 70 (small) an evaporating lotion was applied.

20th April 1824 – There was a slight oozing of blood from the leg; the limb continued hot during the day and the evaporating lotion was continued.

21st April 1824 – She got some sleep during the night. Her pulse this morning was small. She has had no motion, but has taken a dose of castor oil. She complains of not [sic] pain in the part. There is a slight oozing of matter from the lower part of the leg.

22nd April 1824 – Oozing of matter from the lower part of the leg has continued to increase, and a few small vesicles (blisters) appeared on the fore part of the foot, in consequence of which the dressing was slightly loosened in order to favour the return of blood; the tongue was dry and brown: the pulse small and quick a saline draught with a small quantity of Tr: Op: was ordered every four hours.

The report continues along these lines, although the following day the patient was prescribed a small quantity of wine and as generous a diet as she could take.

By the 29th April, the patient is extremely low and discharge from the wound increased in quantity, and of very offensive smell; sight of blackness on front of leg as if the part were threatened with gangrene; wine and porter and stimulating medicines ordered to be continued. As the patient was sinking fast, it was thought the only chance to save her life was to remove the limb. An operation was proposed, she consented and Mr. Travers then said that he would perform it tomorrow at one o' clock.

The following day tells us:

The usual steps of the operation having been completed, great care was taken that as little blood as possible should be lost; three vessels were soon secured, the wound was dressed, and the patient removed from the theatre in 20 minutes from the time she was first brought in. About four ounces of blood were lost. During the operation the patient was quite faint and brandy and wine were administered, which revived her a little.

The patient was pretty easy after the operation; but gradually sank and died on Monday (3rd May 1824). The body was not examined.

✦ OLYMPICS – 1948, THE 'AUSTERITY GAMES' ✦

London has hosted the Olympic Games – considered to be world's greatest sporting event – on three occasions. The first time was in 1908, the second in 1948 and of course the most recent in 2012.

Officially known as the Games of the XIV Olympiad, the 1948 Olympics were completely different to those we know today. For starters, money was tight and the wartime attitude of 'make do and mend' typified the spirit of the Games. Twelve years had passed since the previous competition in Berlin, and Britain offered to host the Olympics for the second time. It was a chance to show the world some of the spirit that won the war.

This was no lavish event and it cost only £730,000 to put together; it was known as the 'Austerity Games'. Only two free tickets were allocated to each foreign embassy. To save money, the gold medals were made from oxidised silver and no new venues were built. This meant female competitors were housed in London colleges, while males stayed in military camps in Uxbridge, West Drayton and Richmond. Local athletes simply stayed at home and commuted to the Games by public transport.

As food and clothing were still under rationing, competitors had to buy or make their own uniforms. The only item of clothing provided free of charge by a sponsor was Y-fronts, with 600 pairs given out in total. The athletes did get extra food rations though, which provided them with 5,500 calories a day instead of the normal 2,600. Many countries helped to increase provisions, with Denmark providing 160,000 eggs and the Dutch sending over 100 tons of fruit.

A rare, hand-drawn 1948 Olympic postcard. (© Private Collection, British Library)

Construction work on the London 2012 Olympic Village outside Stratford International railway station. (Wikimedia Commons © 'mattbuck')

View of the Mall during the 2012 Olympics. (© Jorge Ryan, Royal Parks)

The Games opened in Wembley Stadium on 29 July, with a trumpet fanfare and twenty-one-gun salute. The event was broadcast for the first time on British television, although not many British people had television sets then. Great Britain was the final team to enter the stadium. A medical student, Roger Bannister, who attended the Games as a helper, noticed that the Union Jack flag was missing and ran around to the car park, where he took one from his manager's car and got back with it just in time.

Four thousand, one hundred and four athletes from fifty-nine nations took part and 90 per cent of all competitors were male. Germany and Japan were not invited to participate due to their roles in the Second World War and whilst the Soviet Union was invited, they did not send any athletes.

Fanny Blankers-Koen of the Netherlands was the most successful athlete at the Games. Referred to as 'The Flying Housewife', the thirty-year-old mother took home four gold medals after winning the 100m and 200m races, 80m hurdles and the 4x100m relay. Britain's Dickie Burnell and Bert Bushnell won gold in the men's double skull, the last Olympic gold for rowing for Britain until Steve Redgrave and his teammates won in the coxless four, thirty-six years later. Britain finished the Games with an outstanding twenty medals; three were gold and this saw them achieve a final position of twelfth.

PADDINGTON BEAR AND
‑⁏ THE CROSS-EYED POLITICIAN ⁏‑

It is not that easy to spot the statue of everyone's favourite bear at Paddington Station, because it is quite small and often hidden by people sitting around it. Over the years, Paddington Bear has been burnished to gold by regular attention from children of all ages. He is one of thousands of statues in London; some are great works of art, some slightly weird and others, it has to be said, are just plain ugly. Many portray well-known royal figures, heroes and politicians from around the world.

The most extraordinary is the only 'animatronic' statue in London, called 'Monument to the Unknown Artist' at Bankside on Sumner Street, the official walking route between Southwark Station and the Tate Modern. A plinth approximately 8ft high is topped by the statue of a man dressed in a black suit, carrying a paintbrush. Cameras embedded in his torso mean he will react to passers-by, and mimic their movements and poses. The statue was created by Greyworld, a group of artists who specialise in installations in urban spaces. The sculpture will even strike poses if left alone for a length of time.

Paddington Bear at Paddington Station. (Wikimedia Commons, photographer 'mattbuck')

A statue of journalist and politician John Wilkes stands on Fetter Lane. In 1774, he was elected Lord Mayor of London and he introduced the first motion for Parliamentary reform in 1776. He led a campaign for press freedom, resulting in his imprisonment in the Tower of London. Somewhat unfairly, he was occasionally called 'the ugliest man in England'; a closer inspection of his statue allows you to see that his statue is cross-eyed. However, this nickname did not stop him from womanising and he was a member of the notorious Hellfire Club, a hedonistic club popular with some of the elite in the eighteenth century. When the Earl of Sandwich warned him that he would die either at the gallows or of the pox, Wilkes sarcastically replied, 'That depends, my Lord, on whether I embrace your mistress or your principles.'

William Hogarth's engraving of John Wilkes. (Wikimedia Commons)

Abraham Lincoln's assassin, John Wilkes Booth, was a distant relative.

One of London's oldest statues is that of King Charles I, sitting on his horse on the southern side of Trafalgar Square. Credited as being London's oldest equestrian bronze, the statue was cast in 1633, during King Charles I's reign, at the behest of Richard Weston, who was one of the King's most influential and favourite advisors. In 1649, a brazier called Rivett was ordered to destroy it, but he buried it in his garden and allegedly made money by selling souvenirs from the metal. Eventually, it was given back to Charles II and erected on its present site in 1767.

The distinctive statues of the bluecoats mark the site of charity schools. Many date back to the mid-sixteenth century, with the costumes part of the normal school attire of the period. Blue was used for charity school children because it was the cheapest dye available for clothing, with socks dyed in saffron as that was thought to stop rats nibbling the pupils' ankles.

The smallest sculpture in London is on Philpot Lane in Eastcheap and is of two mice eating cheese positioned halfway up a building.

⚜ PANCRAS WELLS ⚜

In the seventeenth century, the waters of the spa near St Pancras Old Church, which is now partly covered by St Pancras Station, was advertised by the proprietor of the Horns Tavern as being 'an antidote against rising of the vapours also against the gravel.' In bills issued by the proprietors, it was stated that the quality of its waters were 'surprisingly successful in curing the most obstinate cases of scurvy, king's evil, leprosy, and all other breakings out of the skin.' Admission was 3*d*, not a small sum in those days.

In summer, dancing was held several times a week and by 1769, it had become a tea garden supplying 'syllabubs, milk and hot loaves'. 'Dinners and neat wine, curious punch, Dorchester, Marlborough and Ringwood beers and other fine ales and cyder' were also provided. The gardens were extensive and set out with avenues to walk in. A notice dated 10 June 1769 said that, 'Two long rooms will dine two hundred compleatly [*sic*].' However, by the time Daniel Lysons wrote his *Environs of London* (1792–6) the spa had closed and the well was part of a private garden.

⚜ PENNY FOR THE GUY ⚜

Guy Fawkes was a soldier who left his native Yorkshire to fight for the Spanish armies facing Protestant rebels in the Spanish territories. A renowned explosives expert, he was approached by a group of Catholic extremists back in England, who were planning the Gunpowder Plot. By 1605, English Catholics had suffered fifty years of repression. Catholic worship was illegal in England and fines were imposed on all those who failed to attend Anglican services. Some Catholics, including those who approached Fawkes, thought direct action against the government was justified and necessary.

The idea was to blow up King James I of England and VI of Scotland, the Royal Family and the assembled ruling classes of England at the State Opening of Parliament on 5 November 1605. After eighteen months of careful planning, the plot was foiled with just hours to go. Magistrate, Sir Thomas Knyvert got wind that something was amiss and went down into the crypt. He found thirty-six barrels of gunpowder stacked directly below where the King would have been sitting the following day. When asked to explain the situation, Fawkes responded, 'One of my objects was to blow Scotsmen back to Scotland.' Fawkes was arrested at midnight on 4 November 1605.

He was held prisoner and tortured at the Tower of London. Torture was technically illegal and James I was personally required to give a licence for it to be carried out. While just the threat of torture was enough to break the resolve of many, Fawkes withstood two days of terrible pain before he confessed. His signature on his confession was that of a shattered and broken man, the ill-formed letters telling the story of someone who was barely able to hold a quill. However, his fortitude impressed James I, who said he admired Fawkes' 'Roman resolution'. Along with the other conspirators, he died the traditional traitors' death and was hanged, drawn and quartered.

The custom of children collecting money for a stuffed effigy comes from the following old rhyme:

> Penny for the guy,
> Hit him in the eye,
> Stick him up a lamppost,
> And there let him die.

Since that day, before every State Opening of Parliament, normally held in November, Yeomen of the Guard search the cellars of the palace. This is a traditional precaution against any similar attempts against the monarch.

As the nursery rhyme states, 'I see no good reason, why Gunpowder Treason should ever be forgot.'

⚜ PIG-FACED WOMAN OF MANCHESTER SQUARE ⚜

In late 1814 and early 1815, a rumour swept through London that a pig-faced woman was living in Manchester Square. She was supposedly young and wealthy. Reports said she occasionally ventured out of the house in a carriage, her face covered by a veil. Some reports told of a snout protruding from a window, or a silhouetted pig's head in a passing carriage. She was said to eat from a silver trough and grunt instead of speak. It was claimed that her attendant, although paid an annual salary of 1,000 guineas (about £68,000 today), had been too frightened to continue working for her and had resigned, selling her story to the press.

On 9 February 1815, an advertisement appeared in *The Times* from a 'young Gentlewoman', offering to be the pig-faced lady's companion:

> For the attention of GENTLEMEN and LADIES.—A young Gentlewoman having heard of an advertisement for a person to undertake the care of a Lady who is heavily afflicted in the face, whose friends have offered a handsome income yearly, and a premium for residing with her 7 years, would do all in her power to render her life most comfortable, and undeniable character can be obtained, from a respectable circle of friends: an answer to this advertisement is requested, as the advertiser will keep herself disengaged. Address, post paid, to X.Y. at Mr Ford's, baker, 12 Judd-street, Brunswick-square.

Manchester Square. (© Gilly Pickup)

Legends about pig-faced women originated in Holland, England and France in the late 1630s. The stories told of wealthy women whose bodies were normal, but who had faces that looked like pigs.

In the earliest form of this story, the woman's appearance was the result of witchcraft. The magical elements gradually vanished from the story and the existence of pig-faced women began to be treated as fact.

The common belief in these disfigured women led to unscrupulous showmen exhibiting such women at fairs. These were not real women, but animals dressed in women's clothing. As time went on, belief in pig-faced women declined and the last significant work to treat their existence as genuine was published in 1924. Today the legend is almost forgotten.

⚜ POOR FANNY AND A PLETHORA OF ROMAN BUSTS ⚜

These are only a few of the odd items in Sir John Soane's museum, a superbly eccentric monument to his genius. Not only is this Britain's smallest national museum, but this self-endowed monument to London's most illustrious architect and collector, is its most unusual. His sense of the bizarre merges with his brilliance, a remarkable combination that resulted in the creation of a crypt in the basement, evoking an atmosphere reminiscent of ancient Roman burial chambers. The Sepulchral chamber contains Pharoah Seti I's sarcophagus, pharaoh of Egypt (BC 1303–1290), one of the most important Egyptian antiquities ever discovered. Carved out of a single piece of Egyptian alabaster, a calcite limestone, it was originally discovered in Egypt's Valley of the Kings by Giovanni Balzoni, whose original claim to fame was that he was a circus strongman. Soane bought the sarcophagus in 1824, after the British Museum decided it was too expensive for them at £2,000.

When it arrived at his home at 12 Lincoln's Inn Fields, Soane was so jubilant that he threw three evening parties to celebrate his purchase. Whenever Soane had guests for dinner, he usually had tea with them afterwards in the rather melancholy atmosphere of the Gothic-style Monk's Parlour. In his thank you letter to Soane, one delighted guest wrote, 'It was the finest fun imaginable to see the people come into the library after wandering about below, amidst tombs and shafts and noseless heads, with a sort of expression of delighted relief at finding themselves among the living and with coffee and cake.'

Soane's intention was to express 'the poetry of architecture' and there is a proliferation of mirrors throughout the house, while every nook, niche and cranny is crammed with sculptures. Add to this magnificent trompe l'oeil, domed ceilings, cosy narrow passages, elegant rosewood Cantonese chairs inlaid with mother-of-pearl, segmental arches, medieval vases, domes and paintings, it is easy to see he achieved his objective.

His 'Shakespeare Recess' is a shrine to the playwright located at the curve of the staircase leading up to the first-floor drawing rooms. There is a cast of the original bust, which is housed in the parish church of Stratford-upon-Avon and pictures by Henry Howard, illustrating

The Dome Area at night. (© Sir John Soane Museum)

Shakespeare's plays and characters. The drawing rooms themselves were decorated in 'Turner's Patent Yellow', the most fashionable shade of the day. Not surprisingly, when taking into account Soane's eye for perfection, all the upholstery matched precisely. Mrs Soane used these rooms for entertaining and an entry in her diary states: 'Mr Soane out of town … had a dance.'

Soane was born in Goring-on-Thames in Berkshire in 1753, to a family of modest means. This bricklayer's son became not only a superb architect and rival of John Nash, but also a collector of beautiful objects, including Hogarth's *The Rake's Progress*. Described as one of the most inventive of Greek revival architects, he left his legacy in a visually rich and pioneering collection.

He trained under George Dance and Henry Holland, before entering the Royal Academy in 1771. In 1778, he won a travelling scholarship, which enabled him to go to Italy. While in Rome, he met builder Frederick Hervey, Bishop of Derry, and later they were to travel together to Ireland, but as Soane was unable to find work there, he returned to England to establish a modest practice. By 1788, he had gained the important commission of architect to the Bank of England. By then it was obvious that he was a profoundly original architect. Unfortunately, between the two world wars, when the growth of London's workforce reflected the continuing expansion of banking, insurance, trading houses and government, the Bank of England solved its shortage of space by gutting Soane's single-storey bank and replacing it with a vast building by Herbert Baker. This act was described as 'the worst individual loss suffered by London architecture in the first half of the twentieth century.'

Soane married and had two sons, John and George. In 1792, he bought number 12 Lincoln's Inn Fields in London's Holborn, in which he housed both his family and his collection. He hoped his sons would follow his example to become architects, but neither did; his eldest, John, had no interest in architecture, whilst his younger son, George, led a debauched existence womanising and gambling. In his diary, Soane described his sons as 'unnatural' and 'flinty-hearted'. When his wife died in 1815, he declared that George's behaviour had contributed to her death.

His mania for collecting meant that finding enough space for his ever-increasing horde of paintings and objects was a dilemma. Not one to be deterred by a lack of space, he found the ideal solution by buying the house next door in 1813. In 1823, the same year that his eldest son John died, he expanded again by buying yet another house, this time at 14 Lincoln's Inn Fields. The room that houses his picture collection was constructed on the site of the stable yard. In addition to Hogarth's works, there are fifteen etchings by Piranesi and portraits of Mr and Mrs Soane. He designed the room to give the illusion of extra space by using hinged walls, which open like stage curtains.

The inscription on a headstone in the Yard of the Monk's Parlour in the Crypt, at the bottom of the narrow staircase leading from the Picture Room reads

'Alas, Poor Fanny!' This typically English folly is the resting place of Mrs Soane's beloved lapdog, Fanny.

Even today, more than 180 years after his death, Soane still has the ability to inspire and delight those who view his work. He was knighted in 1832, and the following year an Act of Parliament was passed that pronounced his house to be a national architecture museum. Soane continued to amass objects – in his lifetime he collected almost 10,000 books and lived alone until his death in 1837.

Although the museum was open to the public in Soane's day, visitors were not admitted 'in wet or dirty weather'. Visitors are now admitted, whatever the weather, between Tuesdays and Saturdays.

✤ PUNCH & JUDY AND THE ROYAL OPERA ✤

In the seventh century, the area around Covent Garden and the Strand was a busy Saxon trading port called Lundenwic, which was abandoned during the Viking invasion in the ninth century.

In the 1630s, land formerly belonging to Westminster Abbey called 'the Convent Garden' was redeveloped by the 4th Earl of Bedford, with the creation of the first public square in the country. This was the work of the Earl of Bedford, who acted as the developer, Charles I, who gave his strong support to the scheme, and Inigo Jones, one of the most important architects of the day. The piazza was a public space, but the imaginative approach led to its downfall and those that occupied the houses around the square soon began to get annoyed with the lack of privacy. The result was that the rich started to move to newly fashionable areas, including Soho and Mayfair, leaving Covent Garden to a more bohemian populace.

The fruit and vegetable market in the square started in a small way in 1649, but expanded when the Great Fire of London destroyed the City markets in 1666. By the 1760s, the market occupied much of the piazza. With the many theatres in Drury Lane and Bow Street, along with the number of public houses, the neighbourhood acquired a dubious reputation. Eventually, the area was dominated by the market. The main building in the piazza, which is still there today, was erected in 1830, but did not have a glass roof. Gradually, other market buildings were added. The first part of the Flower Market opened in 1872, now the site of London Transport Museum and the National Theatre Museum. More significantly, the market spread to cheaper premises in Seven Dials, in those times a notorious slum area. In these premises, traders operated outside of the main market, or else just used them as warehouses. It was evident that this fruit and vegetable market could not remain in such a congested part

Covent Garden fleshmonger, 1790s. (Wikimedia Commons, photographer A. Dent)

of London, however, it was not until 1974 that the decision was taken to move the market to Nine Elms on the south bank of the Thames, leaving behind empty buildings and vacant premises.

The Royal Opera House, built in 1732 and a major performing arts venue, was erected on the site of the Theatre Royal. After being repaired and expanded in 1787, the theatre burned down. The second Theatre Royal in Covent Garden opened in 1809 with a performance of Shakespeare's *Macbeth*, followed by a musical entertainment called 'The Quaker'. The actor-manager John Philip Kemble, raised seat prices to help recoup the cost of rebuilding, but the move was so unpopular that audiences disrupted performances by beating sticks, hissing and shouting. The riots lasted for over two months until the management was forced to give in to the audience's demands.

In 1856, another fire destroyed the theatre and it had to be rebuilt once again. The theatre became the Royal Opera House in 1892 and was used for pantomimes, recitals and political meetings.

During the First World War, the Ministry of Works requisitioned the building for use as a furniture repository, and during the Second World War, it became a dance hall. The Royal Opera House reopened on 20 February 1946, with a performance of the ballet, *The Sleeping Beauty*.

The first Punch & Judy show recorded in England was performed in Covent Garden in the mid-1600s. Samuel Pepys mentions enjoying it in his diaries. It was

The Royal Opera House. (© VisitLondon / BritainonView / Stephen McLaren)

Mr Punch puppet. (© Fred Tickner / Victoria & Albert Museum of childhood)

rather different from today's version and was performed in a small sideshow tent with marionettes.

⤜ PUTTING ON THE RITZ ⤛

Before The Ritz was built at 150 Piccadilly, the site was home to The Old White Horse Cellar, which was one of the most famous coaching inns in England. Later, the Bath Hotel and then the Walsingham House Hotel, which was demolished to make way for The Ritz, occupied the site. The design of the hotel is the work of architects Charles Mewès and Arthur Davis.

They drew up a French chateau-style masterpiece with a host of interesting details, such as light wells that allowed natural light to penetrate rooms with no outside windows, projecting dormer windows and tall chimneys. Some details are less functional and the copper lions on the corner of the roof are decorative. Mewès designed the interiors with a Louis XVI theme incorporating all of César

The Long Gallery, around 1960. (© Ritz Hotel)

Ritz Hotel. (© VisitBritain / Ingrid Rasmussen)

Ritz's requirements: double-glazing, sophisticated ventilation system, a bathroom for every guestroom, walk-in wardrobes and brass beds.

Leading off the lobby is the Long Gallery, a mass of gilded niches and frescoes, which runs almost the whole length of the building. The absence of walls or doors means it is possible to see all the way to the end. Off the Long Gallery are many of the hotel's key rooms, all with their own fascinating histories. The restaurant, described as one of the most beautiful dining rooms in Europe, features so many chandeliers that the ceiling had to be reinforced to cope with their weight.

Throughout its illustrious history, The Ritz has played host to many prominent figures, such as King Edward VII, King Alfonso of Spain and Queen Amélie of Portugal, Russian Prima Ballerina Anna Pavlova (who danced there), the Aga Khan, and Paul Getty. Charlie Chaplin also visited but needed forty police officers to escort him through the crowd of fans. Noel Coward immortalised the hotel in a song, 'Children of the Ritz', while American actress Tallulah Bankhead sipped champagne from her slipper during a press conference at the hotel in the 1950s. During the Second World War, the Marie Antoinette Suite was used as a venue for Summit Meetings attended by Churchill, de Gaulle and Eisenhower.

On Monday, 8 April 2013 at 11.28 a.m., The Right Honourable Baroness Thatcher, arguably Britain's greatest post-war Prime Minister, died of a stroke in this hotel. Since an operation in December, she had become increasingly frail and spent the final months of her life in a suite here. Adrian Barclay, chairman of the Telegraph Media Group, whose family owns the Ritz, said, 'We were delighted to have the opportunity to play a small part in looking after this remarkable lady in the last few months of her life. Lady Thatcher was one of Britain's greatest ever Prime Ministers and we were honoured to have her stay at the Ritz'.

The bells of Big Ben and the Great Clock at the Palace of Westminster were silenced as a mark of respect during Lady Thatcher's funeral. This was the first time that the bells had been silenced in this way since the funeral of Sir Winston Churchill in 1965.

Lady Thatcher was the longest-serving British Prime Minister of the twentieth century – from 1979 to 1990 – and also the only woman to have held office.

QUEEN WHO BARED
⸙ HER BOSOM TO AN AMBASSADOR ⸙

In 1597, Queen Elizabeth I was sixty-five and had been on the throne for thirty-nine years. That year Andre Hurault-Sieur de Maisse, the French ambassador to Elizabeth's court, was granted an audience that he had been seeking for some time. When his request was granted, the new ambassador travelled from Dover to London, referring to the journey as 'wild'. His boat sailed up the Thames to the palace at Whitehall, where he was ushered into an antechamber. Along with other expectant visitors, he was told to wait until summoned.

After some time, the Lord Chamberlain came along and took him to the Queen, who was sitting in a chair looking melancholy. The ambassador described her as an ageing, wrinkled, almost toothless woman wearing a red wig and revealingly dressed.

Hurault-Sieur de Maisse's account continues:

> After I had made her my reverence at the entry of the chamber, she rose and came five or six paces towards me, almost into the middle of the chamber. I kissed the fringe of her robe and she embraced me with both hands. She looked at me kindly and began to excuse herself that she had not sooner given me audience, saying that the day before she had been very ill with a gathering on the right side of her face, which I should never have thought seeing her eyes and face: but she did not remember ever to have been so ill before. She was strangely attired in a dress of silver cloth, white and crimson, or silver 'gauze', as they call it. This dress had slashed sleeves lined with red taffeta, and was girt about with other little sleeves that hung down to the ground, which she was forever twisting and untwisting. She kept the front of her dress open, and one could see the whole of her bosom and passing low, and often she would open the front of this robe with her hands as if she was too hot. The collar of the robe was very high, and the lining of the inner part all adorned with little pendants of rubies and pearls, very many, but quite small. She had also a chain of rubies and pearls about her neck. On her head she wore a garland of the same material and beneath it a great reddish-coloured wig, with a great number of spangles of gold and silver, and hanging down over her forehead some pearls, but of no great worth. On either side of her ears hung two great curls of hair,

almost down to her shoulders and within the collar of her robe, spangled as the top of her head. Her bosom is somewhat wrinkled as well but lower down her flesh is exceeding white and delicate, so far as one could see.

He continued:

As for her face, it is and appears to be very aged. It is long and thin, and her teeth are very yellow and unequal, compared with what they were formerly, so they say, and on the left side less than on the right. Many of them are missing so that one cannot understand her easily when she speaks quickly. Her figure is fair and tall and graceful in whatever she does; so far as maybe she keeps her dignity, yet humbly and graciously withal.

⚜ QUIRKY GREENWICH ⚜

Greenwich has been declared a World Heritage Site and is home to the Greenwich Mean Time and the Prime Meridian line. It brims over with famous landmarks: the *Cutty Sark*, National Maritime Museum, the Royal Observatory and Sir Christopher Wren's Old Royal Naval College.

King Henry VIII was born at Greenwich Palace on 28 June 1491, the second son of Henry VII and Elizabeth of York. He became heir to the throne on the death of his elder brother, Prince Arthur, in 1502 and was succeeded in 1509. This is where he married two of his wives, Catherine of Aragon and Anne of Cleves. His daughters, who became Queen Mary I and Queen Elizabeth I, were also born here.

Greenwich Park is the oldest of London's eight royal parks and has been associated with royalty since at least the fifteenth century. The area covered by the

The *Cutty Sark, Greenwich.* (© VisitLondon / BritainonView)

park was once occupied by the Romans, evident by the remains of a building, possibly a temple, near Maze Hill Gate. Queen Elizabeth's oak tree, located here, dates back to the twelfth century. King Henry VIII liked to sit under this oak tree with Anne Boleyn, while as a child, Elizabeth I enjoyed playing beside it. Although the tree died in the nineteenth century, the patchwork of ivy that had grown around it held it upright for a further 150 years, until 1991, when a storm almost felled it. Today, it is almost horizontal.

In 1613, King James I gave the palace and park to his wife, Queen Anne of Denmark, as an apology for swearing at her in public when she accidentally shot one of his favourite dogs. Queen Anne subsequently commissioned Inigo Jones to design what is now known as the Queen's House, where a mysterious presence is said to linger. It was even captured on film by a Reverend Hardy in 1966, while climbing up the Tulip staircase. The last time anyone reported seeing the ghost was in 2002.

King James II was the last monarch to use the palace and park. His daughter, Queen Mary II, donated the palace for use as a hospital for veteran sailors and the park opened to them in the early 1700s. The hospital later became the Royal Naval College and the National Maritime Museum later moved onto the site.

Greenwich also found fame when the skeleton of a whale the size of legendary Moby Dick was discovered on the beach buried under mud. Archaeologists unearthed the remains, which had sadly been butchered for its valuable oils and 'bones' sometime between the mid-eighteenth and early nineteenth century. Zoologists estimated that when it met its cruel fate in the Thames it was between fifty and a hundred years old. It is possible that it was harpooned in the Thames Estuary, or beached itself on the Essex or Kent banks, before being towed to Greenwich where it was butchered. It is rare for whales to enter the Thames Estuary, although sometimes they become disoriented and stray far from their usual habitats. It is said that the mammal came from the far northern Atlantic, between Spitsbergen and Greenland.

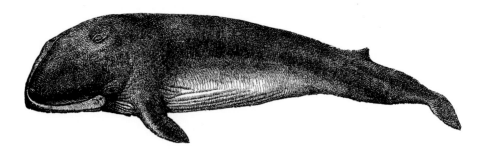

The First Shop in the World. (© VisitLondon / BritainonView)

The Painted Hall has been described as the 'finest dining hall in Europe' and was designed by Sir Christopher Wren and Nicholas Hawksmoor. It was originally intended as an eating space for the naval veterans who lived at the Royal Hospital for Seamen. After his death, Nelson lay in state here. More than 15,000 people came to pay their respects and many more were turned away.

The shop at number 25 Nelson Road, Greenwich, which sells nautical memorabilia, claims to be the first shop in the world. It bills itself as such due to its location at $^4/_{10}$ of a minute west of the Prime Meridian line at Greenwich.

❧ RACOONS, LIONS AND BEARS ❧

The Tower of London was home to the Royal Menagerie for around 600 years. Exotic animals were given as royal gifts, and animals were kept for the entertainment and curiosity of the court. Owning rare animals was a sign of status and power. It was closed by the Duke of Wellington in the 1830s and the remaining animals became part of the founding collection of London Zoo.

Life for the animals was not easy, and they had to survive long journeys by sea and cart to reach the Tower. The Menagerie keepers tried to keep the animals alive, but often they did not know how to look after them properly. They were often kept in poor conditions and cramped cages, and given food that was not part of their natural diet.

The first royal beasts to arrive at the Tower came from Europe and North Africa; they included lions, polar bears and an elephant. In later years, the variety of animals increased to include tigers from Asia, alligators from the Americas, kangaroos and ostriches. Henry III was given a polar bear in 1251 as a gift from the king of Norway. The bear was given a long chain so that it could fish in the Thames.

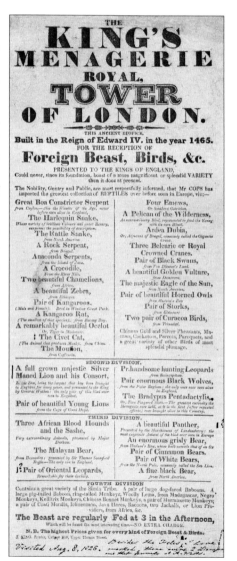

An advert for the King's Menagerie at the Tower of London. (© Historic Royal Palaces)

Among the animals that could be found at the Royal Menagerie in 1829 were leopards, cheetahs, African bloodhounds, Javanese civets, a grey ichneumon, racoons, bears, monkeys, baboons, kangaroos, llamas, eagles, macaws, emus, pelicans, an alligator and 100 rattlesnakes of varying lengths.

THE KANGUROO.

Macropus major. Shaw.

Kangaroo from the Royal Menagerie, 1829. (© Historic Royal Palaces)

Many of the animals were given names. In 1603, a lioness called Elizabeth died during Queen Elizabeth I's final illness. It was seen as an omen that the Queen would also die. On 11 January 1660, Samuel Pepys recorded going to visit a lion called Crowly, 'who has now grown a very great lion and very tame.'

In 1686, a woman named Mary Jenkinson got too close to a lion. Apparently she had been stroking its paw when it caught her arm 'with his claws and mouth, and most miserably tore her flesh.' Surgeons amputated her arm, but she died soon after.

The 1800 guide to the Tower of London listed a lioness called Fanny, one called Miss Fanny, and two more called Miss Fanny Howe and Miss Howe, so-named because they were born on 1 June 1794, the day of Admiral Howe's victory over the French. In 1811, the Hudson Bay Company gave a grizzly bear called Martin to George III, and in 1828, a Bengal lion called George arrived.

⚜ RAVENS IN THE TOWER ⚜

Legend tells that if the ravens leave the Tower of London, the monarchy will fall. According to tradition, the prophecy can be traced back to Charles II, the 'Merry Monarch' (1660–1685). When Charles set up the Royal Observatory at the Tower of London, housed in the north-eastern turret of the White Tower, the Royal Astronomer, John Flamsteed, complained that the birds were interfering with his work. Charles ordered that they should be disposed of, but was told by a soothsayer that if the ravens left the Tower, the White Tower would collapse and a great disaster would befall the kingdom. After hearing the warning, the King ordered that at least six ravens should remain at the Tower at all times. The birds' wings are now routinely clipped, so that they cannot escape and ravens are now a protected species in Britain.

The birds are cared for by one of the Yeoman Warders, otherwise referred to as 'Beefeaters', whose job title is the Ravenmaster. There are seven ravens at the Tower today, the required six plus one spare! They eat 6oz of raw meat and bird formula biscuits soaked in blood each day, they also like an egg each once a week and are said to like fried bread. Apparently, two ravens, called Odin and Thor, who were brothers, used to mimic the Ravenmaster's voice, repeating 'Come on then!' and 'Good morning'. Sadly, these two birds died in 2003.

When a bird dies, it is buried in the Raven Cemetery by the Ravenmaster. The cemetery is in the drained moat close to the Watergate and the St Thomas Tower. There is a Raven Memorial Headstone listing all of the ravens buried there from 1956 onwards.

During the Second World War, the grim raven prophecy almost came true as only one raven was left at the Tower. The other birds were killed by bombing or died of shock during the Blitz. In fact, the ravens' cages are built on the ruined foundation of the Main Guard tower, which was destroyed on 29 December 1940 by a Nazi incendiary bomb. In 1944, the gutted Main Guard building was demolished, revealing the medieval wall of the Innermost Ward. When the Tower reopened to the public on 1 January 1946, there were six ravens once again.

❖ RED TUNICS, RED BREECHES AND PLUMED HATS ❖

The Yeoman Warders, or 'Beefeaters', have long been symbols of London. Their nickname comes from their position in the Royal Bodyguard, which permitted them to eat as much beef as they wanted from the king's table. These men were appointed to guard prisoners and attend the gates. A detachment of the 'Yeomen of the Guard', they have formed the Royal Bodyguard since at least 1509, with their origins stretching back as far as the reign of Edward IV (1461–83).

Today, they still wear the costumes of that period. Their striking uniform is a red tunic with purple and gold lace trim, red knee breeches, red stockings, a ruff, plumed hat, a spear with an ornate base mounted on a long pole and a battleaxe, with a red-and-gold tassel and an ornamental sword.

There are over thirty established Yeoman Warders, who are recruited from the Royal Marines, the Army and the Royal Air Force. These men are responsible for the security of the Tower of London and its visitors, and must

Yeoman Warder at the Tower of London. (© BritainonView)

have received the Long Service and Good Conduct medal before taking up the post. The current contingent of warders will have experienced serving in conflicts throughout the world, including Northern Ireland, the Falklands and Afghanistan.

They conduct public guided tours of the Tower during the day. Every evening, the Ceremony of the Keys is held when the outer gates of the fortress are locked and the keys taken to the Resident Governor. All Yeoman Warders live with their families in private homes in the grounds of the Tower.

⚜ RHYMING SLANG ⚜

Now let's take a 'butcher's' at some words and phrases made famous by cockneys in London's East End, probably invented by street traders in the 1840s. They replaced a common word with a phrase that rhymed with it. This meant that they could chat to one another without their customers being able to understand them.

For instance, 'face' would be replaced by 'boat', because face rhymes with 'boat race.' Similarly, 'feet' would be 'plates', for 'plates of meat'. Sometimes the full phrase is used, for instance 'currant bun' meaning the 'sun'. If someone mentions 'daisies', they are referring to their boots – 'daisy roots'.

Some common phrases are:

'apples and pears' – stairs
'Barnet Fair' – hair
'dog and bone' – phone
'butcher's hook' – look

'I got to me mickey, climbed the apples and the dog went. It was me trouble telling me to fetch the teapots,' translated is: I got to my house (Mickey Mouse), climbed the stairs (apples and pears), when the phone (dog and bone) rang. It was my wife (trouble and strife) telling me to fetch the kids (teapot lids).

By the mid-twentieth century, rhyming slang expressions incorporated names of personalities of the day, especially actors and performers. Take for example 'I've cricked me Gregory Peck' meaning 'neck', or 'I've sent off the Gregory Peck' meaning 'cheque'. A 'Ruby Murray' was a curry. The slang is still used today and 'Do you like these Tony Blairs?' refers to 'flares'.

⚘ RULES: LONDON'S OLDEST RESTAURANT ⚘

Thomas Rule was somewhat wayward, but he promised his despairing family that he would say goodbye to his unruly past, settle down and open an Oyster Bar in Covent Garden. By 1798, it started to attract London's high society and was one of the trendiest venues in the City. Contemporary writers raved about its 'porter, pies and oysters' and the 'rakes, dandies and superior intelligencies who comprise its clientele.'

Throughout its history, Rules has been frequented by literary talents including Charles Dickens, William Makepeace Thackeray, John Galsworthy and H.G. Wells. The late John Betjeman, then Poet Laureate, described the ground floor interior as 'unique, irreplaceable and part of literate and theatrical London.' In its 200 years, spanning the reigns of nine monarchs and entering its fourth century, only three families have owned it.

Actors who have passed through Rules are legendary, and across the decades the restaurant has been an unofficial 'green room' for the world of entertainment, from Henry Irving to Laurence Olivier. Cinema has contributed its own distinguished list of names and one could have seen Buster

Rules Restaurant. (© Gilly Pickup)

Keaton, Charles Laughton, Clark Gable, Charlie Chaplin and John Barrymore at the restaurant.

On the first floor, by the lattice window, was once London's most celebrated table for two. It was the favourite spot for the Prince of Wales, who would become Edward VII, to wine and dine the feisty and beautiful actress, Lillie Langtry. There are whispers, though unconfirmed, that Edward once succumbed to a bad oyster, a rumour that caused the restaurant to be blackballed by society for quite some time. The Prince of Wales is reputed to have had a hearty appetite, so it would have been hard to pinpoint whether the food poisoning originated from Rules.

A talking point in the restaurant today, which is famed for serving traditional British food and specialising in classic game cookery, is an oil painting by John Springs, which features the late Prime Minister, Margaret Thatcher, standing triumphantly in Britannia mode with the Falkland Islands in the background.

S

⁂ SEX, WIGS AND RAGS FOR SALE ⁂

Rosemary Lane, commonly called Rag Fair, was a seething mass of noise, with raucous vendors, an overpowering stench, thieves and vagabonds. The area was mentioned in Alexander Pope's *Dunciad* as 'a place near the Tower of London, where old clothes and frippery are sold.' Much of the clothing sold in this Whitechapel market had been stolen and the rest was rags. Many who came to the fair in the hope of getting a 'halfpenny bargain' were dressed in tatters. A book written in 1878 by an unknown author, *Wonderful London: Its Lights and Shadows of Humour and Sadness*, states, 'there is an atmosphere about old clothes rather distasteful to the uninitiated nostril.'

Prostitutes also plied their trade at the Rag Fair and sashayed among the crowds, carrying baskets of pancakes and dumplings, offering oysters and sex. It was said, 'It's a rare place for a miser to lay his lechery at a small expense, for twopence

Rag Fair by artist Thomas Rowlandson (1756-1827). (Wikimedia Commons)

will go as far here in woman's flesh as half a crown at Madam Quarles's, and with much less danger of repenting his bargain.'

In 1728, washerwoman Mary Coe returned from work to find that her door had been broken open and her possessions were gone. She gathered several neighbours and they went to Rag Fair, 'and was no sooner got there, but they heard a woman crying, "Who will buy a frying-pan, a pair of tongs, or a poker?"' The items were those stolen from Mary. The thief was captured, convicted and transported. In 1733, a court deposition stated that when a draper in Holborn discovered that forty-three pairs of stockings had vanished, his immediate response was to send a boy to look for them at 'Mr Hancock's in Rosemary Lane, opposite the Chequer almshouse.'

A good description of the area can be seen in this entry in the *Daily Gazetteer* of 2 August 1736:

> Late on Friday night, and early on Saturday morning, a great disturbance happen'd in Rosemary-lane, near Rag-fair, where upwards of 150 men assembled in a riotous manner with clubs, and other unlawful weapons, and oblig'd all the house-keepers in Rose-mary-lane, and the parts adjacent, to put lights in their windows, otherwise they would pull their houses down, which put the people in the greatest consternation; so that the whole place appear'd with lights at each window; and some few that had none, got their windows broke to pieces.

People visited the market to buy old wigs, which were primarily sold by Sir Jeffrey Dunstan (1759–1796), a well-known character of the day. Dunstan was a dwarf with knock-knees and a disproportionately large head, who made his living by supplying dealers with second-hand wigs. William Hone's *Every-Day Book* (1826) recalled,

> When Sir Jeffery raised the cry of 'old wigs', the collecting of which formed his chief occupation, he had a peculiarly droll way of clapping his hand to his mouth, and he called 'old wigs, wigs, wigs!' in every doorway. Some he disposed of privately, the rest he sold to the dealers in 'Rag-fair'.

When the fair was in full operation many would wear 'full bottom' wigs and it was not uncommon to hear seafaring persons, or others exposed to the cold, exclaim, 'Well, winter's at hand, and I must e'en go to Rosemary-lane, and have a dip for a wig.' This 'dipping for wigs' was nothing more than putting your hand into a large barrel and pulling one up – if you liked it you paid your shilling, if not, you dipped again, and paid sixpence more. They were also used by curriers to clean waste from the leather.

Eventually, Rag Fair was no more and Rosemary Lane was renamed Royal Mint Street in 1850.

⁣⁣ SMALLEST POLICE STATION IN BRITAIN ⁣⁣

At the south-east corner of Trafalgar Square, unnoticed by most visitors, is Britain's smallest police station. This small box could accommodate up to two prisoners at a time, although its main purpose was to hold one police officer. It was built in 1926, so that the Metropolitan Police could keep an eye on demonstrators, as Trafalgar Square has long been a centre for protests. It was fitted with a door, an interior light and a phone line that connected directly to Scotland Yard to call for back-up. Whenever the phone was picked up, the ornamental light fitting at the top of the box started to flash, alerting any nearby officers on duty that trouble was near. Today the box is no longer used by police and its purpose is as a storage cupboard for Westminster Council cleaners.

⁣⁣ SMOKERS UNITE ⁣⁣

In the past, smoking was one of the few pleasures for the poor. When King James I, a staunch anti-smoker and author of *A Counterblaste to Tobacco*, tried to curb the habit by slapping a 4,000 per cent tax increase on tobacco in 1604, it proved a failure and London had in the region of 7,000 tobacco sellers by the early seventeenth century. The supposed medical properties of smoking were boosted during the Great Plague of 1665–66 when the pungent smoke was thought to protect against disease. At the height of the plague, smoking was made compulsory at Eton public school.

THEIR MUTUAL SPARK!

Cigarettes cartoon advertisement from *Pick Me Up*, 1891.

In the late Victorian period, smoking cigarettes or pipes was largely an urban trend among creative types and art students, and considered a trendy pastime of the day. Upper-middle-class London women's clubs provided smoking rooms for their members. Edith Vance, in a letter to the *Daily Mail* in 1898, called for women smokers to band together in a 'League of Women Smokers'.

However, not everyone thought that women smokers were a good thing. On 10 December 1901, R.D. Blumenfield wrote in his diary:

> I remember going to Vienna about ten years ago to be shocked at the sight of several women smoking cigars. We appear to be progressing towards that end here. After dinner last night at the Carlton I saw four women in the lounge smoking cigarettes quite unconcernedly. One of them had a golden case. Dr Gunton, who was with me, told me that most women now smoke at home. 'That's what makes them so nervy,' he said, 'but when I tax them with over-smoking they nearly always deny it'.

ST PETER'S HOSPITAL FOR STONE ✢ (AND OTHER URINARY DISEASES) ✢

St Peter's Hospital was founded in 1860, in a house at 42 Great Marylebone Street, now 34 New Cavendish Street. Up until then, there was no specialist hospital for urological illnesses. Its purpose was described as, 'The relief of the poor suffering from stone and other urinary diseases, both as In- and Out-patients'. The pamphlet listed twenty-four beds available for men, two for women and six beds in the paying ward. It also stated that no letter of recommendation was required.

The hospital moved to Berners Street in 1863 and changed its name to St Peter's Hospital for Stone, before moving again to Henrietta Place. In 1929, an adjacent house was bought as sleeping quarters for nurses. This house once belonged to Jane Austen's brother, Henry. However, by 1950, rats had invaded the house and the nurses refused to stay there any longer. The Board of Governors sold the building to the Institute of Urology, whose architect supervised extensive interior alterations. There are now three hospitals, known collectively as St Peter's Hospitals.

✢ SWEENEY TODD AND HIS MEAT PIES ✢

Eighteenth-century 'Demon barber' Sweeney Todd allegedly robbed and murdered over 150 customers who came to his shop for a shave or a haircut, and is now considered to be one of history's most prolific serial killers. His unsuspecting clients sat in his barber's chair, which was poised over a trapdoor. After he cut their throats, they dropped into a room below where Margery Lovett, Todd's lover, was waiting to cook their flesh. Sweeney would use a type of razor that would later become known as a 'cut-throat' razor.

Sweeney was born on 16 October 1756, at 85 Brick Lane. Brick Lane was then a rural country lane leading out to the brickfields of Bethnal Green. In 1770, when he was fourteen, Todd was sentenced to five years in Newgate Prison after being wrongly accused of stealing a pocket watch. When in prison he met an old barber named Elmer Plummer, who was serving ten years for fraud. Plummer taught Sweeney how to cut hair, shave, and pick pockets. Sweeney became Plummer's apprentice, shaving some prisoners who could afford their services.

After his release in 1775, with some cash he had stolen while at work in Newgate, he opened his barber's shop at 186 Fleet Street. The shop was beside a narrow alley called Hen and Chicken Court, at the corner of Fetter Lane.

It is said that customers were seated in a revolving chair in the centre of the small shop, placed over a trapdoor leading to a disused cellar. When turned over, the chair would reveal an identical empty chair to take its place. Sweeney would exit through the rear door and down a flight of stairs to where the customer would now be lying.

Sweeney and his lover are said to have made meat pies from their unfortunate customers' flesh. Lovett was probably not solely responsible for baking the pies though, as an account states that she hired a girl and boy who helped with the preparation. It was unlikely either of them suspected where the meat came from.

Sweeney Todd was hanged in January 1802. After his execution, his body was given to medical research by a group of hospital surgeons, so Sweeney ended up, like his victims, with his entrails on a plate. As for Margery Lovett, she cheated death by the hangman when she was found poisoned by prison warders in her cell at Newgate Prison.

Thomas Peckett Prest was probably the first to write the tale of Sweeney Todd and Margery Lovett shortly after their arrest and trial. He had worked on Fleet Street and knew of Lovett's two-storey pie shop. Prest described the shop as:

> a most celebrated shop for the sale of veal and pork pies that London had ever produced. High and low, rich and poor resorted to it; its fame had spread far and wide; and at twelve o'clock every day when the first batch of pies was sold there was a tremendous rush to obtain them … Oh, those delicious pies. There was about them a flavour never surpassed and rarely equalled; the paste was of the most delicate construction and impregnated with the aroma of delicious gravy that defied description.

Sweeney Todd – truth or fiction? You decide.

T

⚜ TAKING THE WATERS AT STREATHAM ⚜

The mineral waters of Streatham Spa were discovered in 1659 and by the eighteenth century, they had become popular enough to make Streatham Common the home of one of Britain's most famous spas. The village had remained largely unchanged until then, but the natural springs gave a boost to the area, celebrated as they were for their health-giving properties.

The waters had been discovered by a ploughman who, not put off by its 'mawkish taste' found it to be good for 'worms' and for 'the eyes'. The reputation of the spa and improved turnpike roads attracted wealthy City of London merchants to build their country residences in Streatham. Concerts were held at the spa and it became a popular place to visit.

All the excitement surrounding the waters meant that people flocked every day to Temple Bar and the Royal Exchange, outlets for the fresh spa water. The suggested dosage was three cups, said to be the equivalent to nine cups of Epsom waters.

Posters proclaimed:

> It is a most valuable remedy for persons labouring under Nervous Debility. List of Diseases in which it has effected permanent Cures:- Eruptions, Scorfula … Palpitation, Giddiness. Sold in Bottles at the Wells at Sixpence per Gallon … Good Accomodation [*sic*] for parties to drink the Water on the Premises. One Penny per Glass …

Dr Samuel Johnson used to visit Streatham regularly in the late 1760s to stay with a brewing family called Thrale. He was a great fan of the mineral water as he thought it helped his gout.

A toll bar at the corner of Thrales' park was where a guard once shot at the Chancellor, Lord Thurlow and Pitt the Younger, because their carriage did not stop to pay the toll.

The spa closed around 1792, but a second mineral spring was discovered. In 1856, a railway station was opened, so people were able to commute between the spa and London. The new railway line made the spa a fashionable resort with the idea of 'taking the waters' for medical purposes growing ever more popular.

⁂ THE OLD CURIOSITY SHOP ⁂

This one-time dairy, on an estate given by King Charles II to one of his mistresses, is the likely inspiration for Charles Dickens' novel *The Old Curiosity Shop*, although it is unlikely this can be proved for certain.

Built in the 1560s, the shop was fortunate enough to escape being destroyed in the Great Fire of London and the Blitz, quite amazing as it was built from the wood of old ships. The building, at 13–14 Portsmouth Street, certainly matches the description of Dickens' half-timbered shop featured in the novel.

In 2007, some newspapers claimed the excitement at the release of the last volume of *The Old Curiosity Shop* was the only historical comparison that could be made to the excitement at the release of the last Harry Potter novel. At the time of writing, the Old Curiosity Shop still functions as a shop and a preservation order protects the building's future and architectural heritage.

⁂ THIEF WHO NICKED QUEEN VICTORIA'S KNICKERS ⁂

Fourteen-year-old Edward Jones broke into Buckingham Palace, sat on Queen Victoria's throne, rummaged in her private apartments, hid under the sofa and stole her underwear. It would have been shocking enough if he had done it just once, but 'Boy Jones', as he was known to the police, broke in three times. Some reports say the intruder disguised himself as a chimneysweep, others say he was simply unwashed.

Of course, in 1838 there was no such thing as royal security. Queen Victoria's court was run on almost medieval procedures, with no particular person directly responsible for her security. 'If he had come into my bedroom, how frightened I should have been,' Victoria wrote in her journal after the boy was discovered hiding underneath a sofa in her dressing room.

After he was caught, his explanation was that he had 'always wished to see the palace' and wanted to write a book about it. Thanks to a clever barrister and a good-natured judge, he was found not guilty of theft at the Westminster Sessions after his first break-in.

Shortly after that, he managed to in break in again, and was caught and given a three-month custodial sentence with hard labour. After he was released, he repeated his crime and found his way back into the palace for a third time. He was arrested in the picture gallery eating cold meat and potatoes that he had stolen from the royal kitchen. Once again, he was brought before the Privy Council and sentenced to three more months in jail.

There was widespread speculation in the press as to how an uneducated boy could enter Buckingham Palace at will. The boy claimed that each time he wanted

Queen Victoria's statue in the gardens of Kensington Palace. (© VisitLondon / BritainonView)

to visit the Queen he had simply climbed in through a lower ground floor window. There was also conjecture as to how many times he had been inside the palace and escaped undetected. His father said that Edward had often been away for many days and when asked what he had been doing, refused to explain his absence.

By that time, Lord Melbourne's government was desperate to get rid of the boy, as they were worried that he might attack or even assassinate the Queen. The decision was made to have him kidnapped and placed on board a ship bound for Brazil. He managed to escape, but was again kidnapped by government agents and made to serve as a sailor in the Royal Navy, without charge or trial. He tried to escape twice, but was recaptured both times and ended up as little more than a galley-boy for six years. Charles Dickens and other humanitarians objected to this illegal treatment, but Queen Victoria and her government would not change their minds. The reason for his eventual release, in 1848, was that they feared unfavourable newspaper publicity if he should die of disease while still a prisoner.

However, Edward continued to break the law and, in 1849, he was convicted for breaking into a house and was eventually transported to Australia, where he found work selling pies. He was not keen on gainful employment though and managed by some means to return to England. After that, his brother persuaded him to return to Australia and he became the city of Perth's official Town Crier.

His palace burglaries echo the more recent exploits of thirty-one-year-old Michael Fagan, who broke into Buckingham Palace in 1982 and managed to get into the bedroom of our present Queen. She woke up to find him sitting on the end of her bed and kept him talking until she could summon help.

TOBY THE SAPIENT PIG
⁂ AND OTHER ATTRACTIONS ⁂

In the eighteenth century, fashionable, wealthy ladies and gentlemen liked to visit London's privately run pleasure gardens; there were about 200 of these gardens at the time. In an age almost as obsessed with celebrities as we are today, the colonnades became the stage for society ladies to show off their finery and be admired. Vauxhall Pleasure Gardens covered around 12 acres and was one of the most popular; it showcased fine musicians and artists. The Prince of Wales visited so often that he had his own pavilion.

When Vauxhall opened, like most gardens, entry was free, but exclusive. Guests needed an invitation and good social connections to get in. However, it changed in 1728 when Jonathan Tyers took over management. He saw a business opportunity in reducing the exclusivity and attracting more people, so he started to charge a one-shilling entrance fee to encourage a broader clientele, but still keep the hoi polloi away.

He added supper boxes, an elegant music room, temples, Chinese pavilions and a fifty-piece orchestra. Entertainment included lion tamers, trampoline clowns, fortune-tellers, ventriloquists, troupes of acrobats, monkeys, deformed human zoo exhibits, battle re-enactments, jugglers and fire walkers. Toby the Sapient Pig was popular with the crowds, because he could apparently read, play cards and read minds. Besides that, he was a mathematical genius and well versed in several languages.

Refreshments were provided and, sometimes, between 5,000 and 7,000 people could eat in an evening. The menu included chicken, ham and beef with custard. Though portions were small and the wine was neither good nor cheap, people still queued to eat here.

As the years passed, the gardens closed due to the owner's bankruptcy, but reopened several times. Many farewell events were held, with a huge fireworks display in 1859 for the last one, after which the furniture was sold. It fetched a hefty £800. After 180 years, Vauxhall Pleasure Gardens were no more.

❧ TYBURN AND LONDON'S SMALLEST HOUSE ❧

London's smallest house is a mere 3.5ft wide and located at 10 Hyde Park Place, dating back to 1805. It forms part of Tyburn Convent. Some believe it might have been built to block a right of way to St George's graveyard in order to deter grave robbers.

Tyburn Convent is home to around twenty nuns, who have taken a vow of silence and still pray for the souls of those who lost their lives on the 'Tyburn Tree', which was London's main execution spot. Fifty thousand people were executed here in the 1700s. The place derived its name from a brook which ran beneath Brook Street, the Tye Bourne and the junction of Tyburn Road (now Oxford Street) and Tyburn Lane (now Park Lane). There is a stone plaque on a traffic island near Marble Arch, which marks the place where the gallows once stood.

This triangular-shaped gallows stood approximately 6-meters tall, its shape meant that each beam could accommodate eight people together, so that twenty-four could swing in one go. As many as twelve hanging days would occur each year. The name given to the leg-twitching movements of the condemned when they were hanging by the neck was the 'Tyburn Jig'.

The gallows remained at Tyburn until 1759, when the official place of execution was transferred to Newgate Prison. Removing the gallows from Tyburn did not please Londoners, as it was considered a good day out to see a hanging. When thief 'Gentleman Jack Sheppard' was hanged, it was said that the event attracted an audience of 200,000 people. He had escaped from prison so often that he was famous, and on this occasion he was carrying a small knife, obviously intended for another (failed) escape attempt.

After they had been hanged, women were publicly burned. Around ten per cent of the women who were hanged had murdered their illegitimate children.

There was a balconied house overlooking Tyburn, and the Sheriffs of the City of London and Under Sheriff of Middlesex would invite guests to watch the executions. They had a good view. Hanging days were declared a public holiday for the labouring classes and the actual day itself was a cause for much excitement. The ceremony began in the morning when the prisoners were handed over to the Under Sheriff. Outside Newgate Prison gates, the crowds would already be arriving as the great

The condemned cell in Newgate Prison.

bell of St Sepulchre, heard only on execution days, would announce the event. Men, women and children would gather to watch the spectacle.

The condemned were taken to Tyburn on a cart, accompanied by the hangman and the prison chaplain. Peace officers would lead the procession, while a troop of soldiers marched immediately behind the cart and a posse of constables would follow on horseback.

The procession passed through Holborn, St Giles and Tyburn Road. Stops made at inns on the way allowed prisoners the chance to indulge in a drink or two, a form of 'Dutch courage', so it was not uncommon for prisoners to arrive at the scaffold drunk.

However, it's not all doom and gloom. In 1705, burglar John Smith was hanged at Tyburn. He had been hanging for fifteen minutes when a reprieve arrived, so he was cut down and revived, as the drop had not broken his neck. He was known afterwards as 'Half-Hanged Smith'.

$\mathcal{U}$

URBAN MYTHS: FROM BLACK SWINE ⁓ TO THE NIGHTCLUB PSYCHOPATH ⁓

Most British towns lay claim to a 'Spring-Heeled Jack' – a character in English folklore known for his ability to jump extraordinarily high because of the springs in his boots. London is no exception and tales abound of this scary character of bizarre appearance, with sharp claws for hands and red eyes which burn and blaze like the devil. Those who claim to have seen him describe him as tall, thin and breathing flames. This urban legend was popular in the Victorian era.

One story goes that in October 1837, a servant named Mary Stevens was walking to Lavender Hill from Battersea. As she walked across Clapham Common, a figure leapt out at her and grabbed her arm. He started to rip her clothes and touched her skin with his claws. She screamed and he fled from the scene. The following day, the same attacker is said to have jumped in front of a carriage, making the coachman lose control and crash. Some of those who witnessed the scene said he escaped by jumping over a 9ft-high wall. News of the weird character spread and soon the press and public named him 'Spring-Heeled Jack'.

His alleged exploits were reported and he became the subject of several Penny Dreadfuls and plays that were performed in the cheap theatres common at the time. For decades, especially in London, he was regarded as a bogeyman, sometimes used as a threat to naughty children.

Another myth centres on Hampstead (NW3), which tells of dozens of black swine living in the sewers beneath the streets. A *Daily Telegraph* report about traditions, published in October 1859, said: 'Hampstead sewers shelter a monstrous breed of black swine which run wild among the slimy feculence …'

Sometimes the swine in the story changed to underground vampires, who fed on a diet of vagrants.

Then there is the legend of the psychopath said to haunt London nightclubs, creeping up behind his victims and injecting them with a syringe. He leaves a note in their pocket, which they find the next morning, informing them that they have been injected with a deadly disease.

There is also purportedly a 'Maniac on the Platform', who lurks among commuters on London's crowded Underground platforms. No one has seen him, but he is believed to be responsible for pushing people in front of oncoming trains.

The 'London Monster' attacked over fifty women between 1788 and 1790. It is doubtful, but at the time the case incited public frenzy. The victims were all attractive and well-to-do, and they reported that a man stalked them, shouted obscenities and in a frenzied attack, assaulted them with blades. Sometimes he would slash their buttocks. On other occasions, he would give them a good kick in the bottom with knives fastened to his knee. He might also ask them to smell a fake nosegay and then stab them in the nose with a spike hidden within the flowers. Unfortunately, he always managed to escape before help arrived on the scene.

Advert for a Spring-Heeled Jack penny dreadful, 8 January 1886. (Wikimedia Commons)

Men, afraid that they would be confused with the attacker, formed an association called the 'No Monster Club', where they wore pins declaring that they were definitely not the monster.

Descriptions of the attacker varied. When it became known that the monster only attacked good-looking females, some unattractive women said that they had been attacked to get attention and sympathy. Some even faked wounds.

Time passed and Londoners were outraged when the London police force failed to capture the man. Philanthropist John Julius Angerstein promised to give a reward of £100 for the capture of the monster and vigilantes began to patrol the streets. Ladies strapped copper pans to their bottoms.

Eventually, a man named Rhynwick Williams was arrested, though he had cast-iron alibis for most of the times the attacks happened. Magistrates still charged Williams with defacing clothing, which carried a harsher penalty than assault.

During the trial, spectators cheered the witnesses for the prosecution and insulted those for the defence. One of the supposed victims, crying, confessed that she had not been attacked at all, and that she had told lies.

The first judge granted Williams a retrial, but he was sentenced for two years for three proven assaults and was made to serve six years in prison. Although the number of attacks lessened after that, they did not stop.

VAMPIRE-LIKE CREATURE, BONE SAWS AND
❖ THE WORLD'S FIRST PORTABLE GRAMOPHONE ❖

The Toy Museum in Scala Street is a museum crammed full of childhood objects and occupies two eighteenth-century houses. The collection of toys dates back to the sixteenth century. Besides many dolls of different types – fabric dolls, china dolls, celluloid dolls, composition dolls – there are doll houses, merry-go-rounds, vintage train sets, puppets and a 4,000-year-old mouse made from Nile clay. Climb up the rickety staircase to see the museum's collection of toy theatres, many made by Benjamin Pollock, the leading Victorian manufacturer of the popular sets. Memories will come flooding back to those old enough to recall Meccano and Bayko building sets, and what is said to be the world's oldest teddy bear, 'born' in 1905.

The Museum of Brands, Packaging and Advertising is off Lonsdale Road in Notting Hill; it has 150 years of culture and lifestyle that come alive through

Some 1940s memorabilia. (© Gilly Pickup)

an array of household products, toys, food, posters, comics, books, technology, royal souvenirs, fashion, design containers and postcards. Consumer historian Robert Opie began his collection in 1963 with a packet of Munchies. His ever-evolving collection of everyday objects now totals over 500,000 items, which tells the story of over 150 years of British consumer society.

Some items are significant in their own right, but many reveal their importance when seen as part of a body of objects unfolding as visitors progress through the museum's time tunnel. Decade by decade, the museum identifies objects which unlock memories; products long since consigned to history. Great inventions of the past are included too: the 1895 Gower-Bell telephone, the 1911 Star Vacuum Cleaner, the 1890 Rippingille oil warming stove and the world's first portable gramophone, the 1909 Pigmy Grand can be seen.

Robert Opie said:

> On 8 September 1963, at the age of sixteen, I bought a packet of Munchies at Inverness Railway Station. While eating them I was struck by the idea that I should save the packaging and start collecting the designed and branded packages which would otherwise surely disappear forever. The Museum houses the highlights of my collection, evidence of a dynamic commercial system that delivers thousands of desirable items from all corners of the world, a feat arguably more complex than sending man to the Moon, but one still taken for granted. The collection has the power to stop visitors in their tracks as they reach a certain part of the Museum's time tunnel and the era which contains their first memories. This could be provoked by a can of Quattro, Texan bar, Kodak camera, children's comic, 1950s jukebox, baked bean tin, packet of tea or bar of soap. Each object has its own significance for every person who enters the Museum.

Ripley's Believe It or Not museum in Piccadilly Circus is filled with over 700 artefacts and astonishing, interactive exhibits spanning six floors. Its creator, Robert Ripley, was an intrepid world traveller, cartoonist, reporter and seeker of the bizarre.

There are Victorian medical devices, including trepanning tools, a gallstone crusher, bone saw and dental key. Victorian surgeons practiced in a very barbaric way and it was thought the more blood on a surgeon's coat the better, as it was considered a badge of honour for them. See a torture chamber with leg and wrist shackles, branding iron and an iron maiden from the sixteenth century, obtained in Nuremburg by Ripley himself, which was responsible for asphyxiating people.

Victorian tunnel. (© Museum of Brands)

Dinosaur eggs. (© Ripley's Believe It or Not Museum)

There is also a picture of Jimi Hendrix painted onto cow dung, a mummified hand and Leonardo DiVinci's *Last Supper* painted onto a single grain of rice.

Discover that Henry VIII loved shoes and ordered sixty-eight pairs, in 1526, to last him six months. These included ten pairs of English leather boots, ten pairs of Spanish leather buskins, one pair of velvet buskins, thirty-eight pairs of velvet shoes in purple, black and crimson, three pairs of black velvet slippers, three pairs of arming shoes, six pairs of English leather shoes, six pairs of shoes in Spanish leather and a pair of football boots.

The notorious Chupacabra (goat-sucker) is a vampire-like creature said to drain the blood of livestock in Puerto Rico, Mexico and the USA. There is a casting in the museum, which was taken after a sighting in rural Florida in 1996. Included in the exhibition is a life-sized knitted Ferrari, an 8ft transformer, a mirror maze, shark jaw and a spinning tunnel.

The Magic Circle Museum (NW1) spills over with historic apparatus, memorabilia, magic tricks, toys, posters and artefacts relating to magicians and illusionists, as well as Europe's largest collection of magic books. See illusionist Chung Ling Soo's robes and learn how he was shot dead during a performance in 1918, view Robert Harbin's original Zig Zag Lady illusion and see rifles used for the 'Bullet Catch', performed by Maurice Fogel in the 1940s. Discover how the British army used a magician to make the Suez Canal invisible to enemy bombers in 1941. There is also an original Sooty puppet with associated Harry Corbett apparatus, sets of props used by television magicians David Nixon and Tommy Cooper, and an audio recording of Harry Houdini taken from an Edison cylinder.

❧ VAULT AT HARD ROCK CAFÉ ❧

Fans of music memorabilia flock to the Vault at the Hard Rock Café on Park Lane. It got its name because the space was once part of Coutts bank and now it holds valuable music mementoes. Items in the collection include the guitar used by Guns 'N' Roses band member Slash in the 'November Rain' video, and, rather bizarrely, one of Madonna's old credit cards, as well as the bustier from her 'Blonde Ambition' tour in 1990. The Vault also has Jimi Hendrix's custom-built Flying V guitar and the first guitar owned by Sex Pistols' guitarist, Glen Matlock. This is the instrument on which he composed their punk anthem 'Anarchy In The UK'. Fans can also see a Western-style shirt worn by the inimitable Keith Moon of The Who from the 1970s, Buddy Holly's glasses and Sting's Fender Precision Bass used in the 2001 video for 'After The Rain Has Fallen'. John Lennon's hand-corrected lyrics for 'Imagine' can be viewed along with the harpsichord used by The Beatles to record 'All You Need Is Love' and 'Lucy In The Sky With Diamonds', from the 1967 album Sgt. Pepper's Lonely Hearts Club Band.

Jimi Hendrix's Flying V Gibson guitar at the Vault on Park Lane. (Wikimedia Commons, photograph by Mike Cattell)

❧ VE-DAY CELEBRATIONS ❧

When Her Majesty the Queen was still Princess Elizabeth, she joined the crowds to celebrate VE-Day on 8 May 1945. In her diary, she wrote, 'Trafalgar Square, Piccadilly, Pall Mall, walked simply miles. Saw parents on balcony at 12.30 a.m. – ate, partied, bed 3 a.m.!'

German General Jodl signed the unconditional surrender document ending the greatest conflict ever to envelope Europe on 7 May in Reims, France. The fighting would cease at 11.01 a.m. the next day, ending six years of bloodshed, though rumour of the anticipated surrender had been circulating for days. The Home Office issued a circular before any official announcement that instructed the nation on how they could celebrate: 'Bonfires will be allowed, but the government trusts that only material with no salvage value will be used.' The Board of Trade did the same: 'Until the end of May you may buy cotton bunting without coupons, as long as it is red, white or blue and does not cost more than one shilling and three pence a square yard.'

There were two celebratory false starts, one on 28 April and another on the morning of 7 May. Then at last came the news that everyone had been waiting for, the official announcement of the end of the war was broadcast at 7.40 p.m. on 7 May.

Soldiers and girls dancing on a London street to celebrate VE-Day. (© IWM London)

The Ministry of Information made a short proclamation: 'In accordance with arrangements between the three great powers, tomorrow, Tuesday, will be treated as Victory in Europe Day and will be regarded as a holiday.'

Within minutes, tens of thousands of people gathered on the streets of Central London to celebrate – Parliament Square, Trafalgar Square and Piccadilly Circus were filled with joyful crowds while boats along the Thames sounded their horns in celebration. For some reason, the most popular song sung in Trafalgar Square was Charles Coborn's 'Two Lovely Black Eyes'.

The next day the streets of London once more spilled over with people. Bands played, flags flew and fireworks lit the skies. At Buckingham Palace, Prime Minister Winston Churchill stood on the balcony with the Royal Family overlooking an ecstatic crowd. The city brimmed with unbridled joy.

Winston Churchill.

The last official event of VE-Day was a broadcast to the nation by George VI. Buckingham Palace was floodlit for the first time since 1939, and two searchlights made a giant 'V' above St Paul's Cathedral; a highly symbolic gesture for a city that had spent years in blackout. People built street fires out of whatever flammable materials they could find. Witnesses reported that London had the same red glow that it had during the Blitz, but this time it was in celebration. Some fires inevitably got out of hand and the London Fire Brigade had to put out the blazes.

The police reported that there was barely any criminal activity throughout the day despite the boisterous behaviour of tens of thousands of people. In the early hours of 9 May, the celebratory illuminations in London were turned off. After all, the war in Japan was still not finished, but for one short day between the evening of 7 May and the early hours of 9 May in a long, tragic and bloody six years, people were able to let their hair down.

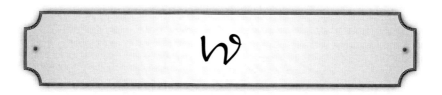

⚜ WELSH HARP RESERVOIR ⚜

The reservoir, which straddles the boundary between the boroughs of Brent and Barnet, takes its name from a public house called the Old Welsh Harp, which stood nearby until the early 1970s. The reservoir is said to contain enough water to fill 3 million baths and today is designated a Site of Special Scientific Interest.

In the 1820s, there was insufficient water to supply the Grand Union Canal and the Regent's Canal, so under a Parliamentary Act, the Regent's Canal Company dammed the River Brent to create a reservoir. William Hoof constructed the reservoir and a bridge between 1834–35, for which he received the sum of £2,740 and six shillings. Construction was not without its problems though, and in August 1835, a few months before completion, four brothers named Sidebottom drowned in an accident. Additional building was completed in December 1837 to extend the reservoir. Then in 1841, after seven days of continuous rain, the dam head collapsed and two people were killed. After that, a supervisor was employed and a cottage near the dam came with the job, so that they could oversee the work.

During the second half of the nineteenth century, the area became a destination for recreation and evening entertainment, almost entirely due to W.P. Warner (1832–1899), who in 1858 became licensee of the Old Welsh Harp tavern. Warner, who fought in the Crimean War, created the tavern along the lines of the London Pleasure gardens. For forty years, he made the Old Welsh Harp one of London's most popular pubs and it was celebrated in song by music hall star Annie Adams.

Amusements were focused not just on the inn, but also around the reservoir. Warner operated a racetrack until a Parliamentary Act made it illegal and the first greyhound races with mechanical hares took place in 1876. In 1891, there was an attempt by French semi-professional balloonist, Louis Capazza, to launch his patented parachute balloon, but unfortunately, the balloon slipped out of the net and launched without him. These activities attracted a mixed crowd, and crime and violence were not uncommon. One observer described the races as a 'carnival of vice'. The reservoir was also famous for Bank Holiday fairs.

The reservoir is now an important site for birds; the Great Crested Grebe, Shoveler, Tufted Duck and Common Tern have all been recorded here. During its early days, it attracted two black-winged stilts, in 1918; the first great white egret to be seen in London, in 1997; blue-winged Teal, in 1996, and penduline tits, in 1996 and 1997. Remarkably, for an inland site, it also attracts rare warblers, with the most significant being an Iberian Chiffchaff in 1972, the first to be recorded in the UK.

The reservoir has a sailing centre and, in 1960, it hosted the Women's European Rowing Championships.

WESTMINSTER ABBEY:
⚜ CORONATIONS WITH MEAT PIES AND WINE ⚜

Benedictine monks first came to this site in the tenth century, establishing a tradition of daily worship that continues today. The present church, founded by Henry III in 1245, is one of the most important Gothic buildings in the country, a treasure house of paintings, stained glass, textiles and other artefacts. The Abbey is a 'Royal Peculiar' (or Royal Peculier), a place of worship which falls directly under the jurisdiction of the British monarch, rather than under a bishop.

The Abbey is the final resting place of many monarchs and has been the coronation church since 1066. Before that date, there was no fixed location for coronation ceremonies and Bath, Canterbury, Kingston-upon-Thames and Winchester had all been used to crown monarchs. There have been thirty-eight coronations in Westminster Abbey, the most recent being that of Queen Elizabeth II, on 2 June 1953.

William the Conqueror, who, as Duke of Normandy, defeated Harold at the Battle of Hastings in October 1066, marched to London with his army after the battle and, possibly to reinforce his claim as King Edward's legitimate successor, chose the Abbey for his coronation on Christmas Day. However, hearing whooping noises and thinking they may have a rebellion on their hands, Norman soldiers set fire to a number of houses nearby. This is thought to be the first definite crowning of a king at Westminster and all subsequent coronations have taken place at the Abbey. Only Edward V, a boy king and one of the Princes in the Tower, and Edward VIII who abdicated, have not been crowned.

The plan of the Abbey copies the French coronation church, Reims Cathedral, in placing the quire to the west of the crossing and transepts. This created a large space between the quire and the sanctuary making it suitable coronation ceremonies.

From at least the thirteenth century, the monarch made a formal progress from the Tower of London to the Palace of Westminster on the eve of the coronation. On the day of coronation, the ceremonies began in Westminster Hall and then a grand procession made its way to the Abbey for the service, returning to the Hall afterwards for a lavish banquet. These ceremonies no longer take place. James II declined the procession from the City, while the preliminary ceremonies and banquet in Westminster Hall were abandoned after George IV's coronation in

Westminster Abbey. (© VisitBritain / BritainonView)

1821. For the coronation of William IV in 1831, a temporary building was erected at the west end of the Abbey to provide space for the processions to form.

The coronation service, though always following a common pattern, also proved remarkably adaptable. The Latin order of service of the Middle Ages was abandoned when Elizabeth I was crowned in 1558, in favour of a mixture of Latin and English, and at the coronation of James I (James VI of Scotland) in 1603, to an English liturgy. In 1689, the service was adapted again so that William III and Mary II might be crowned as joint monarchs.

At eighteenth- and early nineteenth-century coronations, public spectacle sometimes overshadowed religious significance. George III's coronation, in 1761, had a real party atmosphere. There were so many carriages en route to Westminster Abbey that many of them collided. George and his wife, Charlotte, were carried separately in sedan chairs before being escorted into the Abbey on foot, each under a canopy. In those days, the streets were filthy with sewerage and were frequently impassable except by sedan chair.

When the crown was placed on George's head, a huge cheer went up from the boys of Westminster School and the rest of the congregation. When the Archbishop of Canterbury climbed into the pulpit to deliver his sermon, the congregation started to eat the cold meat and pies and drink the wine that they had brought with them. There was lots of noise, chattering, laughing and the clatter of utensils. George III remains the longest reigning king in British history at fifty-nine years, three months and two days.

The coronation banquet was held in Westminster Hall after the service. Hungry spectators in the galleries sent baskets on ropes down to the more privileged attendees at the tables sitting below, who sent them back up filled with chicken drumsticks and flagons of wine.

Subsequently, George IV's coronation was a theatrical spectacle and the King spent vast sums of money on making it as flamboyant as possible. In contrast, his successor William IV had to be persuaded to have a coronation and spent so little money that it became known as 'the penny coronation'. With Queen Victoria's coronation in 1838, however, came a renewed appreciation of the true significance of the coronation ceremony.

Edward VII's coronation, originally set for June 1902, was postponed until 9 August that year. As mentioned previously, Edward had a huge appetite and when European royals arrived at Buckingham Palace in advance of the ceremony on 21 June 1902 a gargantuan feast was laid on, which proved almost too much even for Edward, who collapsed with acute appendicitis and was immediately operated on in one of the rooms at the palace. The remaining food was given to the poor.

When the coronation finally took place, the aged and practically blind Archbishop of Canterbury had the prayers printed in large letters on cardboard, so that he was able to see them. He still misread some of the words, and as the

'The Greatest Show on Earth' by S.D. Ehrhart, around 1862–1937. The illustration shows the procession for the coronation of Edward VII. Many of those participating are wearing medieval costume. (Library of Congress, LC-DIG-ppmsca-25647)

king was crowned, it seemed as though he was about to drop the diadem, then placed it on the King's head the wrong way round. However, Edward's subjects cheered and had a great day for the second time, because the poor were given eight tons of mutton, oysters, prawns, quail and sole to enjoy.

Twentieth-century coronations combined the solemnity of the religious service with magnificent pageantry and, because of Britain's history as an imperial power, became international occasions. The decision to televise the coronation of the present Queen, in 1953, made it possible for the public to witness the ceremony in its entirety for the first time.

☙ WHERE THERE'S MUCK ... ❧

A 'tosher' was someone who scavenged in the sewers and it was a common in nineteenth-century Wapping for whole families to go down into the sewers, where they would find rich pickings amongst the sewerage including coins, sovereigns and jewellery. The saying 'where there's muck, there's brass' came from the work of the toshers.

In 1851, Henry Mayhew published a volume documenting the life of working-class Londoners. He wrote about 'toshers', these sewer hunters who scoured the tunnels and sieved the waste for bones, metal, coins, cutlery, or anything else that may be vaguely valuable. Toshers could earn as much as six shillings a days (around £40 now) for their work. Even after the tunnels deteriorated and became increasingly dangerous, the toshers biggest fear was rats. Jack Black, 'Rat and Mole Destroyer to Her Majesty' explained to Henry Mayhew:

> When the bite is a bad one it festers and forms a hard core in the ulcer, which throbs very much indeed. This core is as big as a boiled fish's eye, and as hard as stone. I generally cuts the bite out clean with a lancet and squeezes … I've been bitten nearly everywhere, even where I can't name to you, sir.

Rat catchers were hired by the city to prevent the spread of diseases and they were paid a pittance, but their efforts in preventing more disease during and after the Great Stink of 1858 dramatically helped London.

Similar to the toshers were the 'flushermen', employed by the Court of Sewers. They would flush away waste and anything that might block the flow of water in London's new sewer system. This was sanctioned when Parliament was unable to ignore the stench of the Thames and believed that 'all smell is disease'. This new sewer network was one of the century's great engineering achievements and the first section opened in 1865.

Henry Mayhew described them:

> The flushermen wear, when at work, strong blue overcoats, waterproofed (but not so much as used to be the case, the men then complaining of the perspiration induced by them), buttoned close over the chest, and descending almost to the knees, where it is met by huge leather boots, covering a part of the thigh, such as are worn by the fishermen on many of our coasts. Their hats are fan-tailed, like the dustmen's.

Late-Victorian London was famed for its 'halting stations', built after the Public Health Act of 1848, which called for 'Public Necessaries to be provided to improve sanitation'. They cost a penny – quite a lot in those days – from which we get the expression 'to spend a penny'. London's first public toilet was for gentlemen and was located on Fleet Street, and it opened in February 1852. Unfortunately, women had to wait another year before one opened for them.

Though basic, these facilities were a huge improvement to previous centuries, where people simply used a container of some description and then threw the contents into the gutter or the Thames. People who lived above ground level would simply chuck the contents along with a shouted warning of 'gardyloo', from where we get the slang word 'loo', meaning a toilet.

In the twelfth century, if you were caught short in London you could employ the services of a 'human lavatory', which cost a farthing. These men and women wore black capes and carried a bucket. They would protect your modesty with the cape while you sat on the bucket.

In the 1300s, London Bridge's one-room unisex public toilet had several seats and waste dropped straight into the river. In 1339, William Wombe, who had the unenviable task of cleaning the public toilets, drowned in the Thames having gone into the river for a wash.

WINSTON AND THE
❧ EXPLODING CHOCOLATE BAR ❧

The Nazis hatched a plot to kill Sir Winston Churchill with a bar of exploding chocolate during the Second World War. Adolf Hitler had his bomb-makers coat explosive devices with a thin layer of dark chocolate, which they then packaged in expensive-looking black and gold paper. The German idea was to use secret agents to leave the chocolate, which was called 'Peter's Chocolate', in the War Cabinet dining room among other items.

This chocolate was lethal; it was packed with enough explosives to kill anyone within several metres. However, British spies found out about the plot and Lord Victor Rothschild, one of MI5's most senior intelligence chiefs, received a tip-off. His Lordship wrote to an illustrator to get him to draw images of the chocolate, so that posters could be displayed to warn the public to be on the lookout.

In the letter he says:

> We have received information that the enemy are using pound slabs of chocolate which are made of steel with a very thin covering of real chocolate. Inside there is high explosive and some form of delay mechanism. When you break off a piece of chocolate at one end in the normal way, instead of it falling away, a piece of canvas is revealed stuck into the middle of the piece which has been broken off and a ticking into the middle of the remainder of the slab.

In his letter, his Lordship enclosed a rough sketch by someone who had seen one of the bars. He asked the artist to indicate in the text on his drawing that a bomb would go off seven seconds after the piece of chocolate and attached canvas was pulled out.

It is amazing to think that the course of history could have been changed entirely if Winston Churchill had discovered that bar of chocolate.

❧ WOOD STREET COMPTER ❧

The Wood Street Counter, or Compter, was a small prison in Cheapside. Built in 1555, it replaced the Bread Street Compter destroyed in the Great Fire. 'Compters' were controlled by a sheriff and the inmates were not terribly violent or treacherous, they were usually dissenters and debtors though it also held people accused of misdemeanours, including public drunkenness. Under each sheriff was a secondary, a clerk of the papers, four clerk sitters, eighteen sergeants-at-mace, master keeper, and two turnkeys. The words of arrest were, 'Sir, we arrest you in the King's Majesty's name, and we charge you to only us.'

Prisoners could choose which area they would languish in and they had the choice of three. It was only fair that they could choose, after all, they had to pay. The 'Master's Side' was the most expensive, the 'Knights' Ward' a little cheaper and 'the Hole' cheapest of all. The fees were called 'garnish' within the prison system. Visitors came and went as they pleased, and inmates could bribe jailors for favours. Of course, the majority of jails were not like this and were, in fact, filthy and brutal, with prisoners crammed together in tiny cells.

At dinner in the Compter a vintner's boy would fill a bowl with claret and the new prisoner had to drink to the health of everyone there. It cost him money to do this, but there was no option. After a week or two, the prisoner's pockets would be quite a lot lighter than they were on arrival and he would usually have to move across to the Knight's Ward, where living conditions were less salubrious. The move entailed another 'garnish' of 1/6d.

For those in the Hole life was much less comfortable, as the beds were wooden boards arranged above one another on the wall like shelves and came at a cost to prisoners of 1/3d. Of course, the longer a debtor remained in the Compter, the greater his debt would become. If a convicted felon could not find surety for his good behaviour upon release, after his term in prison he remained there as a debtor, sometimes for a longer period than the original prison sentence.

The Compter's Commonwealth (1617) by William Fennor, was a work written from the author's experience of being imprisoned in Wood Street Compter, and is regarded by many historians as one of the principal sources for assessment of English sixteenth-century prison conditions. In his book, he wrote:

> … and if a gentleman stay there but one night, he must pay for his garnish sixteene pence, besides a groate for his lodging, and so much for his sheetes. When a gentleman is upon his discharge, and hath given satisfaction for his executions, they must have fees for irons, three halfepence in the pound, besides the other fees, so that if a man were in for a thousand or fifteene hundred pound execution, they will if a man is so madde have so many three halfepence …

This Compter was still housing prisoners as late as 1727, when the *London Gazette* from 6 July listed thirteen insolvent debtors awaiting court on 25 August.

Although demolished in 1816, its cellar still survives today, gated and padlocked from the public.

King's Bench Prison in Southwark stood from medieval times, until it closed in 1880. Prisoners were often joined by their families. Dickens wrote about it in *David Copperfield*, with Mr Micawber being imprisoned here for debt. In 1828, it was described as 'the most desirable place of incarceration in London'. The courtyard was often full of traders including oyster sellers, barbers and tailors, while the many gin shops on site did a roaring trade. The more affluent prisoners even had a regular cook to prepare their meals.

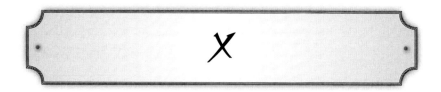

⚜ X-RATED – BROTHELS APLENTY ⚜

From the 1700s to the late 1800s, prostitution was big business in London. In 1857, records showed that one in every sixty London houses was a brothel and one in every sixteen women was a prostitute. The Haymarket was popular with 'ladies of the night' and even though thousands plied their trade, apparently demand always exceeded supply. Tougher laws in the previous century deemed that 'pretty women' (prostitutes) could only sell their charms in certain parts of town. If they went elsewhere, they had to remove the top half of their clothes so that everyone would know what their job was. At that time they could expect to earn two guineas per assignation; earning more than £400 a year. If you consider a housemaid earned only £5 a year, it is not surprising that many women opted for the former 'occupation'.

'Bawds' or pimps, women who were too old to make a living in prostitution, sought out young girls and earned about £150 (around £11,000 today) for selling 'deflowering rights' for a virgin to a nobleman. Bawds would trawl the inns or look for street girls and offer them free accommodation in return for 'respectable work'. They would suffer violence and threats unless they did as they were instructed. Bawds were referred to as 'Hags of Hell' and the most famous bawd of all, Mother Needham, was pinioned in the stocks, in April 1731, for running a house of ill-repute, before being stoned to death by an angry mob.

Each year at Christmas, Samuel Derrick published a directory called *Harris's List of Covent Garden Ladies,* which listed where prostitutes plied their trade. Derrick borrowed the name for his publication from Jack Harris, a waiter who called himself 'The Pimp General of All England.' The two had become acquainted while in Newgate debtor's prison. Thousands of copies of the list were sold.

This publication provided details as to services on offer, fees and a brief description of the women's physical attributes. An extract from the 1788 edition tells us:

> Miss B. Number 18 Old Compton Street, Soho. This accomplished nymph has just attained her eighteenth year, and fraught with every perfection, enters a volunteer in the field of Venus. She plays on the pianoforte, sings, dances, and is the mistress of every manoeuvre

in the amorous contest that can enhance the coming pleasure; is of middle stature, fine auburn hair, dark eyes and very inviting countenance, which ever seems to beam delight and love. In bed she is all the heart can wish, or eyes admire every limb is symmetry, every action under cover truly amorous; her price two pounds.

'Miss Smith' was listed too. She lived in Duke's Court in Bow Street and was described as, 'a well made lass, something under the middle size, with dark brown hair and a good complexion.' The guide was not too kind about Miss Robinson at the Jelly Shops: 'a slim and genteel made girl – but rather too flat.' Meanwhile, Mrs Hamblin, of No. 1 Naked-Boy Court in the Strand, was described as, 'The young lady in question is not above 56 … we know she must be particularly useful to elderly gentlemen who are very nice in having their linen got up.'

Moll King and Betsy Careless were famous prostitutes of the time. They both knew many prominent men, including novelists Henry Fielding and Daniel Defoe. King, who ran a Covent Garden brothel, is believed to be the inspiration for Defoe's heroine, Moll Flanders. Interestingly, Daniel Defoe was born plain 'Daniel Foe' and added the 'De' himself to impress.

Betsy became a teenage prostitute. Her appearance was described as 'deceptively innocent' and she had a nasty habit of passing on her syphilis, before she lost her

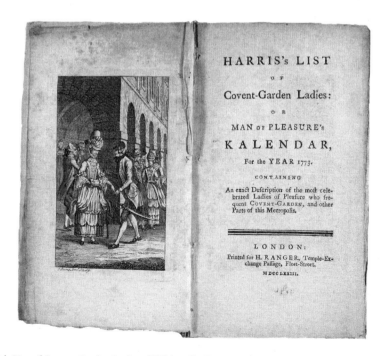

Harris's List of Covent-Garden Ladies. (Wikimedia Commons)

charms and sunk into debt. She died in her early thirties. Her death was recorded in the *Gentleman's Magazine*: 'Buried from the Poor-house of St Paul's Covent Garden, the famed Betsy Careless who helped gay gentlemen of this country to squander £50,000.'

Worried about the effect of widespread venereal diseases upon society, Parliament passed the infamous Contagious Diseases Acts of 1864, 1866 and 1869, which officially allowed prostitution, but 'arranged for the forcible examination of prostitutes for disease', which inevitably meant that all women walking the streets were suspected, whether or not they were engaged in prostitution.

Covent Garden was the centre of a vast sex trade with hundreds of brothels. Fornication in public was common and it cast a murky shadow over everyone as even children were routinely treated for sexual disease. A German visitor observed a nation that had overstepped all others 'in immorality and addiction to debauchery'. English society expected, even encouraged, men to pay for sex. Prejudice barred women from all but menial jobs. Prostitution at least offered financial independence, earning the same per month as a tradesman or clerk would earn in a year. For beautiful and savvy women, the gamble paid off. Child prostitute, Lavinia Fenton, married a duke, but most were destined for disease and early death. Puritanical societies for 'the suppression of vice' encouraged punitive laws against disorderly houses and streetwalking. Writers including Henry Fielding and Samuel Johnson drew attention to the prostitutes' plight.

Theresa Berkely was a nineteenth-century dominatrix, who ran an 'upmarket brothel' in Hallam Street, just to the east of Portland Place. She specialised in chastisement, whipping and flagellation. There are no pictures to let us know what she looked like, though occasional descriptions have said that she was attractive with a strong disposition. Her talents became highly sought after by the aristocracy of the day, meaning that she ran no risk of being arrested or being raided by the police. She offered absolute privacy to protect her clientele and became extremely wealthy.

According to an unnamed source:

Her instruments of torture were numerous. Her supply of birch was extensive and kept in water, so that it was always green and pliant: she had shafts with a dozen whip thongs on each of them; a dozen different sizes of cat-o'-nine-tails, some with needle points worked into them; various kinds of thin bending canes; leather straps like coach traces; Holly brushes, furze brushes; a prickly evergreen called butcher's bush and during the summer vases, filled with a constant supply of green nettles, with which she often restored the dead to life. Thus, at her shop, whoever went with plenty of money could be birched, whipped, scourged, needle-pricked, half-hung, holly-brushed, butcher-brushed, stinging-nettled, curry-combed and tortured.

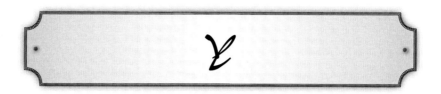

YESTERDAY'S LONDON,
⁖ SWINGING SIXTIES AND CARNABY STREET ⁖

'Ancient elegance and new opulence are all tangled up in a dazzling blur of op and pop.'

Piri Halasz writing in *Time* magazine, April 1966

In the 1660s, the area around what is now Carnaby Street was open fields used by the Court as a hunting ground. The huntsman used the cry 'Soho' rather like the call 'Tally O' and the area became known as Soho Fields. The main features were Oxford Street and Swallow Street, and there was a small lane to the east, which became King Street and later, Kingly Street. Maps of the mid-1600s show a few buildings along Swallow Street, a windmill and a gaming house. Following the plagues of the mid-seventeenth century and the Great Fire of 1666, the pressure to build increased and land to the east became used for Pest Houses and plague pits.

The 1960s saw an end of post-war austerity and London became a psychedelic explosion of colour, fashion, music and new attitudes. Carnaby Street shot to fame worldwide as the hippest place to be; the place to 'hang out' for the young and fashionable, as satirised in the Kinks' *Dedicated Follower of Fashion*. Using the skills of the established Soho 'rag trade', it was the place to buy relatively inexpensive, trend-driven merchandise that mirrored contemporary changes in society and culture.

These necessary changes were due to the baby boom of the 1950s, so the urban population was younger than it had been since Roman times. With the abolition of National Service for men in 1960, young people had more freedom and fewer responsibilities. They rebelled against the limitations and restrictions of post-war society.

Londoners found themselves with more disposable income than ever before and were looking for ways to spend it; weekly earnings in the 1960s outstripped the cost of living by 183 per cent and in London, where earnings were generally higher than the national average, the figure was probably even greater. This combination of affluence and youth led to a flourish in music, fashion, design and anything else that would banish the post-war gloom. Creative individuals

Carnaby Street. (© VisitLondon / BritainonView / Juliet White)

gravitated to the capital, including artists, writers, publishers, photographers, advertisers and film-makers.

Carnaby Street's transformation into a world-famous shopping street began with John Stephen, a clothing entrepreneur who arrived from Glasgow in 1952, aged nineteen. He began his career working for Moss Bros, but started his own menswear workshop on Beak Street in the mid-1950s. He moved around the corner to 41 Carnaby Street after a fire destroyed his Beak Street premises. He sold cheap, but fashionable, clothes for men and became an instant success story. Soon his empire expanded and he owned several shops in the street. By the end of the 1960s, Carnaby Street was London's second most visited tourist attraction after Buckingham Palace.

In contrast to the 1950s, this was the time to wear bright colours, bold patterns and horizontal and vertical lines. Girls wore false eyelashes, heavy eyeliner, pale lipstick and hemlines shot up thanks to Mary Quant who invented the mini-skirt, which spread beyond simple street fashion into a major international trend. The style came in to prominence when Jean Shrimpton wore a short white shift dress on 30 October 1965, at Derby Day, the first day of the annual Melbourne Cup Carnival in Australia, where it caused a sensation. Hemlines kept rising throughout the 1960s, and by 1968 reached well above mid-thigh and were known as 'micro-minis'. Of course, minis meant goodbye to stockings and suspenders, and tights became popular. They provided protection from the elements without the shocking glimpse of stocking tops. Women would not go out with bare legs then. A pair of Wolsey tights cost about £1 in 1965, and with careful daily washing they could be made to last a month.

Unlike the 1950s music scene, which had been dominated by US rock 'n' roll, the 1960s burst upon the public. Groups like the Beatles, Rolling Stones, the Kinks and The Who helped to revitalise British pop. Musicians often pioneered alternative ways of dressing and many dressed in 'mod' outfits – the word stands for 'minimal and modern'. Mods were classy and rode on scooters, usually Vespas or Lambrettas. Mod lifestyle and musical tastes were the opposite of their rival group, the Rockers, who preferred 1950s rock 'n' roll, sported black leather jackets and greased hairstyles, and rode motorbikes.

In 1966, Harry Fox and Henry Moss opened the doors of 'Lady Jane', the first ladies' fashion boutique in the street. Harry Fox went on to add 'Lady Jane Again', 'Lady Jane's Birdcage', a souvenir shop and a menswear shop, 'Sir Harry', to his empire. Stars from around the world made Lady Jane a must-visit on their trips to London, including Jayne Mansfield.

Harry Fox, president of the Carnaby Street Trading Association, lobbied local government to have the first sign, 'Carnaby Street Welcomes the World' hung above the street and later it was pedestrianised. Now, the street's star has faded and it is mainly full of souvenir shops and the odd camera-wielding tourist.

Z

⋇ ZEBRA TALES ⋇

Lionel Rothschild, a member of the famous banking family, admired zebras so much that, in 1894, he harnessed several to a carriage and drove them through the streets of London, then onto the forecourt of Buckingham Palace to prove that zebras could be tamed. Sometimes he also rode a giant tortoise. Rothschild suffered from a speech impediment and was very shy, but had an endless fascination for animals, insects and birds.

At twenty-one, he was made to go to work at the family bank, Rothschild & Sons in London, though he had no interest in a career in finance. In 1908, he was allowed to quit the bank, and his parents established a zoological museum as compensation and financed his worldwide expeditions to seek out animals.

In his lifetime, he assembled the largest collection of fauna ever accumulated by one man. His menagerie included a flock of flightless kiwis from New Zealand that accompanied him to Cambridge when he arrived as a university student in 1887, 144 giant tortoises imported from the Galápagos Islands, a sheep-sized South American rodent called a capybara, wild asses, anteaters, emus and kangaroos. These animals all roamed freely around his Hertfordshire estate.

... AND THE MOST FAMOUS
⋇ ZEBRA CROSSING IN THE WORLD ⋇

The zebra crossing on Abbey Road, St John's Wood became the album cover for the Beatles' Abbey Road album in 1969, and is now Grade II listed. Together with the nearby Abbey Road studios, also listed Grade II listed, they remain a mecca for Beatles fans the world over.

Today, traffic is constantly held up as people try to get photos of themselves recreating the pose on the crossing.

The front cover design, a photograph of the group on the zebra crossing, was based on sketched ideas by Paul McCartney, and was taken on 8 August 1969. At around 11.30 a.m., photographer Iain Macmillan was given ten minutes to take the photograph as he stood on a stepladder and a police officer halted the traffic.

In the scene, the group walk across the street in single file, from left to right, with John Lennon leading, followed by Ringo Starr, Paul McCartney (who has bare feet) and George Harrison. To the left of the picture is a white Volkswagen Beetle, which belonged to one of the people living in the flats across from the recording studio. After the album was released, the numberplate was stolen many times. The car was later sold at auction for £2,530, in 1986, and is on display in the Volkswagen museum in Wolfsburg, Germany.

Bibliography and Sources

❧ BOOKS ❧

Bondeson, J., *Queen Victoria's Stalker* (Amberley Publishing, Stroud, 2010)

Carrier, Rhonda, *Frommer's London with Kids* (John Wiley & Sons Ltd Publishing, United States, 2005)

Cruickshank, D., *The Secret History of Georgian London: How the Wages of Sin Shaped the Capital* (Random House, London, 2010)

Cunningham, P., *A Handbook for London, Past and Present* (John Murray Publishing, London, 1849)

Diamond, M., *Victorian Sensation* (Anthem Press, London, 2003)

Eames, A., *London Insight City Guides* (APA Publications, Washington, USA, 1988)

Flanders, J., *The Victorian City: Everyday Life in Dickens's London* (Atlantic Books, London, 2012)

Gervat, C., *Elizabeth: The Scandalous Life of an 18th Century Duchess* (Century, 2003)

Inwood, S., *A History of London* (MacMillan, London, 2000)

Leapman, M., *The Book of London* (Weidenfeld & Nicolson, London, 1989)

Milne, G., *The Great Fire of London* (Historical Publications Ltd, Kent, 1986)

Pipe, J., *London: A Very Peculiar History* (Book House, Sussex, 2010)

Rappaport, H., *Beautiful Forever: Madame Rachel of Bond Street, Cosmetician, Con Artist and Blackmailer* (Vintage, London, 2010)

Sharp, Dennis, *The Illustrated Encyclopedia of Architects and Architecture* (Quarto Publishing, London, 1991)

Shelley, Henry C., *Inns and Taverns of Old London* (Europaeischer Hochschulverlag, Bremen, 2010, originally published in 1909)

Taggart, C., *The Book of London Place Names* (Ebury Press, London, 2012)

Thompson, A.C., *George II: King and Elector* (Yale University Press, New Haven and London, 2011)

Thomson, B., *The Story of Scotland Yard* (Kessinger Publishing, Whitefish USA, 2005)

Thorold, P., *The London Rich* (Viking, New York, 1999)

Weinreb, B and Hibbert, C., *The London Encyclopaedia* (Book Club Associates, London, 1983)

❧ NEWSPAPERS AND PERIODICALS ❧

Daily Mail
Daily Telegraph
The Economist
The London Magazine
Fortean Times

❧ WEBSITES ❧

www.1stcontactenews.co.uk
www.britainexpress.com
www.british-history.ac.uk
www.cabbieblog.com
www.charlesdickenspage.com
www.coventgardenlife.com
www.crimeandinvestigation.co.uk
www.dailymail.co.uk
en.wikipedia.org
www.english-heritage.org.uk
www.eyewitnesstohistory.com
www.foundlingmuseum.org.uk
www.guardian.co.uk
www.historic-uk.com
www.history.co.uk
www.history.uk.com
www.hrp.org.uk
www.inlondonguide.co.uk
www.ivu.org

www.knowledgeoflondon.com
www.londontheatredirect.com
www.luminarium.org
www.museumoflondon.org.uk
www.nottingham.ac.uk
www.parliament.uk
www.rictornorton.co.uk
www.royal.gov.uk
www.royal.gov.uk
www.royalparks.org.uk
www.spencerhouse.co.uk
www.theanneboleynfiles.com
www.thegarret.org.uk
www.theritzlondon.com
www.victorianlondon.org
www.vintage-toppers.com
www.weird-encyclopedia.com
www.westminster-abbey.org

❧ ARTICLES ❧

Adams, J., 'Take her up tenderly', Times Literary Supplement, 8 August, 1997
'An Audience with Queen Elizabeth I, 1597', EyeWitness to History (www.eyewitnesstohistory.com, 2004)
Carrier, R. Bignell, 'Elephant Man', *The Independent*, 15 August 2012
Fisher, D.R. (ed.), The History of Parliament: the House of Commons 1820-1832, (Cambridge University Press 2009)

www.history.co.uk (Southwark News, January 2010, Sourced from Southwark News archives with thanks to Southwark Local Studies Library and Debra Gosling)

Chronicle of the Grey Friars of London, 1531, www.archive.org

'Whitechapel', Old and New London: Volume 2 (1878), pp. 142-146. www.british-history.ac.uk

'Parishes: Streatham', A History of the County of Surrey: Volume 4 (1912), pp. 92-102. www.british-history.ac.uk

'Westminster: Buckingham Palace', Old and New London: Volume 4 (1878), pp. 61-74. www.british-history.ac.uk

The Independent 'Archaeologists dig up 200 year old skeleton of Moby Dick' by David Keys Sept 2010

Old Bailey Proceedings Online (www.oldbaileyonline.org, version 7.0, 22 October 2012)

'Princes Gate and Ennismore Gardens: The Kingston House Estate', Survey of London: volume 45: Knightsbridge (2000), pp. 157

'Cheapside: Northern tributaries: Wood Street', Old and New London: Volume 1 (1878), pp. 364-374. www.british-history.ac.uk

'The river Thames: Part 1 of 3', Old and New London: Volume 3 (1878), pp. 287-299. www.british-history.ac.uk/report

Wilson, A.N., 'Elizabeth I and the men she loved' www.dailymail.co.uk Aug 20, 2011 Mailonline

'The borough of Southwark: Introduction', A History of the County of Surrey: Volume 4 (1912), pp. 125-135. www.british-history.ac.uk/report

If you enjoyed this book, you may also be interested in …

From 221B Baker Street to the Old Curiosity Shop:
A Guide to London's Literary Landmarks
STEPHEN HALLIDAY

London has been unrivalled as a source of inspiration for writers since the days of Geoffrey Chaucer right through to J.K. Rowling. *From 221B Baker Street to the Old Curiosity Shop* will explore the capital both from the viewpoint of the many writers who have used it as a stage for their plots and their characters.

978 0 7524 7024 5

Bad Companions: Six London Murderesses Who Shocked the World
KATE CLARKE

This book features the cases of six London women, each very different in temperament, age and status, who resorted to murder. Their motives and methods varied. This fascinating study explores the cases of Kate Webster, Catherine Wilson, Sarah Drake, Eliza Fenning, Elizabeth Brownrigg and Catherine Hayes in depth, and reveals whether these women were tragic, misunderstood or *just plain wicked*.

978 0 7524 9364 0

The London Book of Days
PETER DE LORIOL

Taking you through the year day by day, *The London Book of Days* contains quirky, eccentric, amusing and important events and facts from different periods of history, many of which had a major impact on the religious and political history of Britain as a whole.

978 0 7524 7939 2

London's Big Day: The Coronation 60 Years On
DAVID LONG & GAVIN WHITELAW

At the core of this book is a hitherto private collection of more than 200 images showing London's West End on the day of Queen Elizabeth II's Coronation. None have been published before, and together they provide a unique and precious record of this historic occasion – the day of the Coronation as it was seen by ordinary members of the public.

978 0 7524 9714 3

Visit our website and discover thousands of other History Press books.

www.thehistorypress.co.uk